GIANMARIA POLIDORO

Francis
of Assisi

EDIZIONI PORZIUNCOLA

Translation by: *Benet A. Fonk ofm*

Sixth reprint: *January 2017*

ISBN 978-88-270-0370-1

© Edizioni Porziuncola
  Via Protomartiri Francescani, 2
  06081 S. Maria degli Angeli – Assisi (PG)
  Tel. 075.8051498 – Fax 075.8051598
  www.edizioniporziuncola.it

Stampa:
Grafiche VD – Città di Castello (PG)

INTRODUCTION

In order, to look for something new in this book, the reader ought to check out the level of interpretation and also the meaning of that adventure which Francis experienced. In particular, I feel the need to highlight how the saint of Assisi, more than anything else, presented to the world a new, fascinating way to live a really Christian life. Francis' great contribution, in my opinion is how he persuaded society to use the world of the gospel Beatitudes to solve the problems which plague it and to achieve a happy social life. This is what he wanted to tell the world. This is what he tried to exemplify with his life and with his plan of living which was embodied especially in his first followers.

I maintain that Francis of Assisi, primarily known as the founder of religious orders, should be studied as one who began a brand new style of Christian living within the Church of God.

The things I mentioned above are part of what I have learned by reading Francis' life. I did not modify the meaning of words or events. I have just presented my interpretation which has matured over the years as I have become familiar with the person and by developing the habit of paying attention to every aspect of his life.

In this work, of course, I have followed some guiding principles regarding the happenings of history and the interpretation of events, writings, and resources. But this is not the proper place to discuss philosophical foundations and methodologies. Rather, this is the context to verify the results obtained and to receive the inevitable criticism. I must, however, add something I consider necessary:

I have spoken of Francis as someone full of brilliant intuitions about interpreting the Gospel. Now I must say that he was also a person who tried up till the end of his life to explain to himself and to offer to others that which burned inside of him like a fire. In fact, it was difficult for him to focus on anything satisfactorily and to get others to understand what he meant. It is the age-old problem of that expressive capacity, that effective use of language, to make oneself and those intuitions fermenting within oneself clear to others.

Francis was like a person in the middle of a dark forest. He wanted to say something that had not been said before. He wanted to map out a road for himself which, though not yet fully known, was foreseen clearly as the right path to follow. With words that seemed stiff and legal, ascetic and overused to his contemporaries, he tried to clarify for himself and to explain to others a world yet unexplored but already in existence. Just as a bit of fresh water in the hollow of one's hands can ward off time and time again the stifling effect of suffocating heat, so a person like Francis of Assisi – one of those special people who arrives just every once in a while by the grace of God's creative power – brings a refreshing discovery to the intricate tangle of earthly reality.

In order to imbibe a little of this refreshing water, I will speak to you of Francis.

ASSISI TODAY

Assisi today is not exactly the same town as it was at the end of the twelfth century. If you were to take in hand a panoramic photo of the city extending along the foot of Mount Subasio, you would notice an imposing, massive building on the left: the Basilica of St. Francis, started in 1228 with the foundation stone laid by Pope Gregory IX, who had come to Assisi to canonize the saint. In the lower part of town lie the walls of the city, clean among the greenery. These start from the fortress set high above at the top of the mountain, descend steeply embracing the first houses, and then form a border dotted with several towers to protect the city's doors.

These city walls run along the lower part of the town to include the apron of houses enclosed within, pass by a few of the mansions which now block the view of the landscape, and climb quickly upward to the right, leading toward the ruins of the "rocchiciola" (or fortress) which dominates the road that leads to the mountain top. From here, finally, your line of vision returns to the other end of the fortress above the city.

The fortress ("La Rocca") of Assisi formed (even if not completely) and still forms today the hinge or central focus of the city walls. Today, it is true, it is only a shadow of its former self, but it still suggests its ancient splendor. At the end of the twelfth century the fortress and the walls of Assisi formed a beautiful oval shape in which houses, gardens, and churches were enclosed.

Between the fortress and the upper part of the town there lies a steep meadow. It was probably used, in part, to train the horses and, at the same time, to put some distance between the nobility and the ordinary citizens. As a result, the houses in town seem to be clumped together in too tight an embrace, giving the feeling of being suffocated.

In this city the first merchants of the twelfth century built their homes and shops while looking askance at the rich landowners who were proud of their titles and their feudal holdings. As in so many other Italian cities where the first civil liberties were beginning to dawn, the people of Assisi were frequently very close to their bishop, while being afraid of the nobles and imperial troops.

As always, the poor were poor. They served as foot-soldiers and maids in the houses of the wealthy people. As workers they endured the drudgery of the warehouses and dye-works of the wool merchants. As craftsmen they tried to scrape together what little money they could by working themselves to the bone. The most unfortunate ones went about begging for a bit of bread or for a half-day of work. Outside the city, scattered among the isolated cottages and in the basements of the small and large castles, the peasants eeked out a meager livelihood, often living as serfs. In out-of-the-way places the lepers struggled to stay alive, while within the forest the vagabonds and thieves slept in the open air.

When something happened, the news was spread by messengers who shuttled between the various courts and among the different lords, by merchants who traveled from city to city to look for good markets, and also by the monks who sometimes were holy men and sometimes were just wandering do-nothings. The lack of information and the unreliable means of communication were made up for by the close attention which travelers paid to events during their long journeys and by the patient reflection of those who listened with eager ears during those dark evenings in which oil and wicks had to be used sparingly.

Thus was Assisi in the twelfth century when Italy was beginning to reopen its eyes after the exhausting task of transforming the decadence of the Roman Empire by forging new initiatives for society to assert itself.

Among the more adventuresome merchants in the city of Assisi, was Peter, the son of Bernardone. He traveled often, and it seems that he went to France on several occasions to transport merchandise and make some money. (When we speak of "France," we actually mean that section of the country called "Provence.") Going to France from Assisi was a long and dangerous journey because there were no railroads, no paved roads, no effective national police force.

Besides the merchants, and together with them, other people traveled too, like mercenaries, dreamers, and thieves. Some of these were local bandits, and they were particularly active in areas where people had to pass through. Such things, however, did not get in the way of the speedy movement and the strong will of a hearty merchant. Taking these sort of risks, Peter Bernardone built up his fortune and felt the need to start a family. So, one day – whether this is fact or fiction, I do not really know – he returned from France with a wife along with his full cache of goods.

Out of respect for her rich husband, citizens called the young merchant's wife "madonna": Madonna Pica. That is to say, "Lady Pica." Most likely all this took place about 1180 or 1181.

When Peter Bernardone set off again on another journey to

the marketplaces of France, he left the side of his pregnant wife.

Assisi was enjoying a certain political stability during these years, though it still lacked freedom, and this gave a lot of confidence to the genteel Peter who was more interested in social tranquillity than in freedom of thought.

Already in the year 1173 the German emperors had taken possession of the citadel of Assisi, taking it away from the authority of Pope Alexander III. It is true that in 1174 there had been a popular uprising against the imperial power, but the Chancellor of the Empire, Archbishop Christian of Mainz, put it down with the sword, reserving the use of the cross for other situations. For the time being he wore it on his chest as a sign of his episcopal dignity.

Not even on that famous day, May 29, 1176, after the rout of the imperial party in Legnano, where the Lombard Union and its war chariot had demonstrated its power, did the people of Assisi get rid of the Germans who put up a relentless fight in the duchy of Spoleto on which Assisi was dependent. On the contrary, Frederick Barbarossa himself turned up at the city gates and took solemn possession of Assisi. When he went away, he left someone whom he could trust, Conrad of Urslingen, to govern the fortified citadel. The presence of the emperor gives firm testimony to the stability of the imperial rule in Assisi.

So, under these conditions Peter Bernardone left for France. In those days you knew when you started a journey, but you never quite knew when you would return. So, during one of her husband's journeys, possibly in the winter of 1182, Lady Pica gave birth to a beautiful baby boy. In the absence of the father, the baby was called "John," perhaps because the parents had already agreed upon this name. It was a beautiful, traditional name, and did not stand out as novel or unusual.

When Peter returned home, he carried in his heart another name for the son who was waiting for him. Maybe his business in France had been very successful on this particular occasion or maybe the long time he spent walking around, riding a horse, or dreaming about his newborn son had heightened his imagination. Anyway, the first thing he did was to change his name. He called him "Francesco," that is, "Frenchy": Francis. This is what we call him today. This is how he would be known throughout the world for all these centuries.

Francis did not lack a thing. He was born a fortunate fellow, in a fine house of merchants. One day, though, when he was a youth, he did feel that he was missing something in his life, as happens to all rich people; and since wealth was not lacking, he felt it was the absence of a noble title.

So, that baby was born with a good dose of luck on his side. Here was a healthy child with a family of very comfortable means in a quiet and well-to-do city, even though without much freedom. The mother must have been one of those who exhibited much affection in the style of fine, traditional families. His father saw in him the product of a well-bred family, receptive in a trusting way to many future possibilities. In order to give him a better training in view of his future responsibilities as a merchant, Peter sent him to school. Of course, it had to be a school run by priests. In fact, in those days priests and monks were charged with the education of children. Hence, the little Francis attended class at the nearby church of St. George. He was taught just a few things: reading, writing, and arithmetic. The most important was working with numbers; for Peter this was one of the most crucial things.

The boy, moreover, got his first cultural experience through the sacred texts of the Bible and learned to read the Gospel from the worn parchments at St. George's. Besides, at home he learned to do some small jobs and to supervise the workers. His father looked on him proudly. Francis was a lively and intelligent youth. From among the more genteel set, he would turn out to be a top-notch merchant. He showed lots of promise, and Peter was very pleased with this and imagined him at the height of his future activity: with arms full of bolts of damask and with a money-bag filled with shiny gold coins.

This was a dream – one, though, which would not last very long.

RESTLESSNESS FOR SOMETHING NEW

A s far as the childhood and early youth of Francis are concerned, we cannot afford much credibility to the information garnered from his early biographers. In fact, in dealing with this aspect of his life they held to some criteria which today we no longer accept. Since it was necessary to say something about the saint, they believed that the best thing was to describe his infancy and youth from a pietistic perspective or even to offer to the readers a particular moral lesson. Therefore, we cannot trust what they said about Francis as a boy and as a young man.

Francis was one of those youth which today we would call "middle class" with the same flaws and virtues commonly found in the fellows of his social status.

Nonetheless, he seemed to have had a good-natured disposition and a spirit filled with high principles and generosity. School did not occupy all of Francis' waking hours. While the young man was growing up (and people matured quickly in those days), he divided his time between play and school work, as well as beginning to be tutored in his family's business interests. The shop of Peter Bernardone was very well supplied with various fabrics, some of them quite precious. Cheap labor allowed for a certain kind of family-run operation for manufacturing cloth (both weaving and dyeing). It took long hours and was tedious work. Francis lent a hand to help the business get ahead, whether it was accompanying his father to outdoor markets in nearby cities or supervising the workers. The studies he was doing at St. George's were intertwined with manual labor. If this were not so, we would have great difficulty explaining his love for working with his hands which would prove to be so fundamental in his own life-style and in that of his disciples.

When Francis was fifteen years old, Assisi was socially alive. Let us set this against a European background. As long as the imperial authority had been in the hands of the emperor Henry VI, the Empire remained calm, and even Assisi, which was under the rule of an imperial governor, restrained its tensions. When, however, upon the death of Henry, the Empire faced a period of growing weakness (because Frederick was so young and inexperienced and because Otto and even the Pope himself were jockeying for power), the people of Assisi felt that it was time to take action.

It was the spring of 1198. The longings for liberty were being felt even in Umbria where the people were afraid of being subjected once again to the papacy which had already taken over full possession of the Duchy of Spoleto. In order to prevent any possible overlord from being put into a position of authority, the Assisians thought it best to attack the "Rocca Maggiore" (that great fortress overlooking the city), the headquarters of the German governor, and dismantle it. This event set the city on a course of self-determination.

Francis, now sixteen, was all fired up because of these extraordinary events. He was one of those young people who clamored and plotted with a heart full of dreams to live in a city free from the meddling of the emperor's men and aristocrats. The attack on the fortress, in fact, was just the beginning of a journey which would prove to be both exhausting and exciting.

Between the years 1199 and 1200, a war began in Assisi between the people of the middle class on the one side and the nobility on the other. The middle class people won, and a large portion of Assisi's noble families fled in defeat to Perugia to plot revenge. Behind the lovely words of freedom, justice, and honor, as often happens, there lies hidden, even in Assisi, the struggle for supremacy and the acquisition of power. The rich who were not of noble birth thought that their wealth was at least as valuable as a fancy coat of arms, and hence they wanted more say-so since they felt themselves to be a more youthful force.

Among those engaging in battle, there were also the common folk, the "little people," who in general participated by means of the well-heeled members of society in the hope of grabbing whatever they could in the shuffling of the political cards. Some of them, however, sided with the nobles because of long-standing servitude or special interests. Whatever side they were on, they fought their battles for someone else, and they did not seem to count the cost. During these years Francis too experienced conflict and war on the battlefield. This was the autumn of 1202.

The struggle for control of the citizen's power, begun in 1198, had not yet reached any definite resolution. The nobles, it is true, were forced to run away from the town and to take shelter in Perugia. But they had not given in. The exile in Perugia had matured their plans for revenge. Together with the interests of the municipality of Perugia they formed an explosive situation which severely threatened the first stages of liberty in Assisi, which was violently opposed by Pope Innocent III who was not scrupulous about resorting to canonical sanctions.

Conflict on the open field was inevitable. Perugia and Assisi dispatched their respective armies (what an inflated word for such a modest reality!). These clashed midway between the two towns at Collestrada, a small hill which rises up separating the Spoleto Valley from the Tiber Valley. The people of Perugia won the battle and the soldiers from Assisi were imprisoned.

So, after the defeat, Francis was taken to Perugia as a prisoner. His clothes and his armor clearly demonstrated whose son Francis would have been and hence the Perugians sent him to the jail of the knights with the hope of a good ransom.

"Once, while his fellow prisoners were letting themselves go in despair, instead of complaining, Francis showed a cheerful attitude to them, thus revealing his optimistic, jovial nature. One of his companions, then, told him he was crazy to be so cheerful while in jail. Francis answered in a strong voice: 'What do you think I am going to be in my life? You should know that I am going to be venerated in the whole wide world" (3 Comp. 2:4). Were these words only a young man's fantasies or were they prophecies invented with wisdom after the fact? We shall never know.

Meanwhile, in the Perugian prison, Francis was making himself popular with his fellow prisoners. He was the only one who never lost his good humor and who managed to get along well with everybody. Even when one of his mates turned against the others for an insult he had suffered, Francis remained his friend and tried to bring peace among the prisoners. The son of Peter Bernardone spent a whole year in jail. But his health was not that strong, and he soon fell ill. His jailers, out of pity or perhaps more out of their desire for a ransom, set him free and sent him back to Assisi even before the political problems and the rivalry between the two cities had been resolved.

Over a two to three year period, Francis had accumulated a whole gamut of experiences from high elation to deep sorrow: he had endured a war of rebellion and a war of the soul, a struggle on the battlefield and the struggle of imprisonment;

antagonism and disdain, as well as friendship, from among his fellow prisoners. Certainly this was enough to bring a young twenty-year-old fellow to maturity. Relatively quickly he had gone from the feelings of rebellion, to the pride of being a winner and a fighter, to the humiliation of suffering imprisonment, and finally to a point of inner peace which blossomed into serenity of spirit. This spiritual state brought him to transcend the restlessness of the moment and to understand, through experience, that peace was really superior to war and that there was value in rebuilding friendship even with the "proud gentleman" (2 *Cel.* 4) who had created such disunity among the group of prisoners. Consequently, violence was something to be overcome and put aside. He accomplished this not only in an intellectual way, but also in an existential way because he had actually experienced how much better peace was than war.

From what can be gathered from historical sources, the disease which Francis contracted was long and somewhat mysterious (either because of the lack of medical expertise during that time or because of its psychological nature). Regardless, we do not know much about it. It is sure, though, that after the illness Francis was no longer the same young fellow he had been. Experience matured him quite a bit.

When Francis recovered, he went back to his old job, working in his father's shop and going to trade fairs. "One day, while he was in his shop, busy selling some clothes, a poor man came forward and begged him for some money, for God's mercy. Taken by his greed for gain and by his preoccupation to conclude his bargain, he did not pay any attention to the beggar, who then left.

"Immediately, as if he were seized by the grace of God, he reproached himself for being so rude to that poor person. He thought: if that poor man had asked for help on behalf of a grand count or baron, then you would have certainly satisfied him. All the more reason to do so out of respect for the King of Kings, who is Lord to everybody.

After this experience, he resolved never again to deny anything that was requested in the name of such a Grand Lord" (3 *Comp*. 1:3).

"When he was outside, Francis gave money to any poor beggar he met; or, if he did not have any, he gave away his hat or his belt, so as not to send the beggar away empty-handed. If he did not have these, he would take the person aside, take off his own shirt and give it to him. He bought the tools that churches required and secretly gave them to the poorest priests" (3 *Comp*. 3:8).

We who live in an age of great wealth must interpret carefully the real meaning of giving away a hat or a belt or even a shirt. I do not think anyone today would need to pass on an old hat or maybe a dirty shirt to a poor person. Clothes are so plentiful that we do not have to remove an article of clothing off our back to dress the poor. At the time of Francis, however, everything was precious. A shirt, however used or sweaty, was already something of a luxury which not everyone could afford. This is precisely why we so often read about the sharing of clothing as such an act of charity.

"Once he came across a knight who was noble but poor and badly dressed, and he felt a tender pity for his sad condition. So he promptly undressed and let the other man wear his clothes. In this way he accomplished a double charity with a single deed, as he both hid the shame of a noble knight and relieved a poor man from his misery" (*Major Legend* 1:2).

As is clear, the first sign of Francis' inner change seemed to be addressed to the poor. This contact was another of his early experiences which left a deep impression on his spirit.

Francis' life was not made up of only work and reflection. Though there was a change in many of his interests and opinions, he still was considered to be one of the most brilliant

18

young men in town. He was intelligent. He had youthful enthusiasm. He had money. He was popular among his friends.

The young people of Assisi whose families were well-off used to come together every now and then for a party. It was nothing particularly wild, just a fun evening together spent eating and drinking and singing love songs. One night, probably in the spring of 1205, Francis did something to distinguish himself from everybody else. Maybe that evening he picked up the tab for the meal or perhaps he was especially witty. In any case, his friends had chosen him to be the king of the party, and they invested him with royal trappings – a stick was transformed into a scepter for the occasion. When they were all full of wine and happiness, they went outside to sober up a bit. The spring evening was always beautiful, and the youth meandered along the streets of Assisi, through gardens and houses, singing their ballads and teasing each other with cutting humor and sophomoric jokes. Francis was not up front where he was supposed to be. After the first few songs he fell silent and wandered to the back of the group, lost in a strange kind of introspection. It was just at that moment that a completely new experience of being introverted swept over him who was so accustomed to selling goods at the counter. While he was walking along, "all of a sudden the Lord was present to him, and his heart was filled with so much sweetness that he could not move or talk. He did not perceive anything but the sweetness, and all other sensations vanished so that – as he admitted afterwards – no one could have moved him from that place, even if they had cut him into pieces."

His friends soon realized that their "king" was absent. It seemed so strange that he was not there with them leading the fun of the evening. When they saw him at the end of the street all by himself with his mind in another world, they figured the most logical thing one could think in such a situation: Francis had fallen in love. They had to find out who was the beautiful girl he had fallen for. Probably they just had to look up into one of the windows of the nearby homes. They went back to where he was and approached him. They realized that the expression on his face was completely different from what they were accustomed to seeing. "Francis," they demanded, "what is going on in your mind? How come you did not follow us? Are you perhaps daydreaming about getting married?" Francis reacted as if he had just come back from a world all his own. His eyes were filled with a dreamlike wonder which lit up his face. He responded: "Yes, it is true. I was dreaming of taking as my wife a young woman who is nobler, wealthier and more beautiful than any of you have ever seen before" (cf. 3 *Comp.* 3:7).

The authors of the aforementioned "*Three Companions*" interpreted this "*bride*" as the ideal of religious life. Here was one more of Francis' significant early experiences. It was a spiritual feeling.

During the years 1202 to 1205, we come in touch with the restlessness of Francis. It was not just the result of a long and mysterious illness. It was that uneasiness of a person who was not sure of the direction that he wanted to take for his life and was looking for the way. He did not know for certain where he wanted to go, but he felt that some unrecognizable future was calling out to him from the distance.

In this period of discontent he accumulated many experiences. Maybe he had even dreamt of some practical or utopian outlet for his life, but nothing really satisfied him. Ordinary life did not seem to fit the bill. Then why not try a life of adventure? He started thinking about becoming a knight. This was the time of the Crusades, of remarkable tensions, of the troubadour songs about Roland of Roncesvalles. What about becoming a knight? That might be a good idea!

"One night while he was in bed sleeping, Francis had a vision of somebody calling him by name and leading him to a palace of extraordinary magnificence and beauty. The place was filled with weapons and with some splendid shields marked with crosses hanging all around on the walls. He asked his escort in the dream if he knew who owned the shining armor and the gorgeous palace. 'Everything including the palace itself,' said the person in the dream, 'belongs to you and your knights.'

"When he woke up, he tried to explain to himself the meaning of this dream by giving it a worldly interpretation. He had not yet tasted the fullness of the spirit of God, so he still imagined that he would be a magnificent prince. After thinking it over, he decided he would be a knight in order to get to that princedom. Therefore, Francis resolved to join up with Prince Gentile, who was leaving for the area of Puglia, so that be could be knighted by him. So he prepared to outfit himself with precious clothes. Because of this decision he became more upbeat than usual, and everyone began to wonder what was happening. To those who asked him why he had become so happy so quickly, he responded, 'I know that I will become a great prince!'

"He hired a squire, mounted his horse, and set off for Puglia. That night, when he arrived at Spoleto worried about the journey, he lay down on the ground to sleep. While he was dozing off, he heard a voice interrogating him where he was going. So, in response he revealed his whole project. The voice then said, 'Who can treat you better – the lord or the servant?'

"The Lord,' Francis replied.

The person speaking went on to ask, 'Then why are you abandoning the Lord for the servant, the Prince for his subordinate?'

Then Francis said, 'my Lord, what do you want me to do?'

'Go back to your home town to do what the Lord will reveal to you.'

By the grace of God he felt suddenly changed, feeling like a completely different person" (cf. *Anonymous Perugian*, 1:56).

It appeared clear, then, that the secular state was not for him. It was a time of waiting because the various "no's" he received before from his past situations were turning into positive experiences. To find out what was going on, Francis needed quiet and research. After his dream and his return to Assisi, we find the young Francis almost leaning toward the life of a hermit. More and more often he took advantage of the solitude around San Damiano, that tiny and dilapidated little church in the countryside, halfway up that road between Assisi and the valley which leads to France.

He, however, would change this direction of his life, if we can call it that. Francis always made his choices in life when he collided with reality; and reality brought him to choose now what he felt he ought to decide upon, and what would turn out to be best for him.

This was the year 1205.

ON THE ROAD TOWARD FREEDOM

That experience which seemed to be directing Francis toward a hermit's life gave way to a sudden, unexpected burst of vitality and a new interest in the world. In the lapse of time between 1205 and 1206, we do not know which of two significant events had a primary role in upsetting Francis' quiet life as a hermit while he was still brooding over the direction he ought to follow. It was not through meditation, however, that he found this path. He had two extraordinary experiences which would open up for him a very exciting horizon: meeting the leper down on the plain below Assisi and hearing the voice of the crucifix which talked to him at San Damiano's.

Both of these events carried an explosive charge. Both were sudden and very clear in their meaning.

The only thing different about the two happenings was this: the encounter with the leper highlights Francis' free, spontaneous, and active response, while the voice at St. Damiano's underscores his passive or receptive understanding of that which came to him from on high. Practically speaking, these are two different expressions of the very same inspiration for Francis to take action.

Knowing which of these two events was more relevant may be useful in understanding which was the primary or predominant in Francis' definitive choice for taking a new direction for his life. After various considerations, including the psychological impact of the two events before him, I have come to the conclusion that encountering the leper was the most formative or basic experience of his life.

When Francis was close to dying, he felt the need to make out a second testament, one that was more extensive than that which he composed in a hurry in Siena the previous May. He began this second text by saying:

"This is how God inspired me, Brother Francis, to embark upon a life of penance. When I was in sin, the sight of lepers nauseated me beyond measure; but then God himself led me into their company, and I had pity on them" (*Test.* 1-2).

We can put into perspective how important and fundamental this encounter with the leper was when he added: "After that I did not wait long before leaving the world" (*Test.* 4).

This is how the encounter came about: one day Francis went riding by himself in the area around Assisi. Perhaps he went into the valley where there was an old leper colony. While he was riding along lost in thought, a most unpleasant sight brought him back to the real world. There in front of him stood this man with rags for clothes and a swollen face – it was a leper. Francis felt this bitter taste in his mouth. Without realizing what he was doing, he drew up the reins to turn the horse around and run away. This was an instinctive reaction because lepers frightened him to death.

Then he came to his senses. After a moment of hesitation, in an instant, he changed the whole course of his life.

Francis got down from his horse, shuddering from the swift and sweet decision that was born within him. He reached into his pocket for some money and offered it to the poor man who seemed bewildered by so much courage and generosity. Then, once again, there was a surge of power within him. He took the hand of this miserable fellow and pressed it to his lips. With fear and passion he kissed him. Then in a flash he remounted his horse and was off, digesting the heroism which was placed on his shoulders.

"Some days later," as the *Legend of the Three Companions* relates, "he took a large sum of money to the leper hospital, and gathering all the inmates together, he gave them alms, kissing each of their hands" (3 *Comp.* 4:11).

"When I had become acquainted with them, what had previously nauseated me became a source of spiritual and physical consolation for me" (*Test.* 3).

After the encounter and the kiss, Francis was a completely different person. He had set out on a course from which he could not turn back, he had taken an exciting step. He had touched the point of no return.

But why the leper, of all people?

At the time of Francis, lepers were no more than objects of pity and were treated as such. They received alms, but absolutely had no rights whatsoever in society. In fact, they were obliged to separate themselves from society. Before they were cut off from the others, they were provided with a nice funeral in church with the appropriate candles and black pall to signify their social death. After the funeral rite, the lepers became the object of pity, just like any one of the dead for whom the liturgical *requiem* is sung before being buried in a tomb of stones and bricks.

The lepers had no tombstones over their heads, but they did have to carry a bell whenever they left the leprosarium, in order to warn healthy people that they were close at hand. We ought not be scandalized by this behavior. We would have done the same thing. In those days this was perhaps the only way to protect society from contagious diseases.

So, everyone considered it normal that the lepers were shunned and kept at a distance. Well, almost everyone. Unless we really understand what it meant for Francis to embrace a person who was cut off from society with the risk of being marginalized himself because of his action, we cannot fully comprehend Francis' impulsive decision nor his decisive choice.

Days went by, and the young man from Assisi, who was always so ready to take risks on his way to Puglia, was still looking for a new course to give to his life. Until something happened.

Between Assisi and San Damiano's there was a street which went right down the hill through the olive trees. The path which led to San Damiano's wended its way down to the plain where it connected with the ancient Flaminia highway that passed through Foligno and Spoleto on its way to Rome.

San Damiano was the name of an old, dilapidated church. A priest looked after the place. He was one of those poverty-stricken priests who lived a simple life and had little chance to hope for a career. The area around the church, isolated though it was, did not keep him too far away from civilization, and was also an ideal place for meditation. Even today there is something about San Damiano's which invites a person to come by and think.

Francis knew of the little church where there was a certain devotion to an old and heavy wooden cross on which was painted the image of Christ and, on the sides and below, the various personages associated with Calvary. One day, while he was nearing the church, Francis was drawn to enter. Falling to his knees with devotion, he prayed intently before the cross, and said:

"Most High, all glorious God, enlighten the darkness of my heart. Give me right faith, certain hope, and perfect charity, with deep humility, wisdom, and understanding, that I may know and do your most holy will. Amen."

Perhaps this prayer, among the various writings of St. Francis, can offer us a better insight into that meeting with God which took place in the dark shadows of San Damiano's.

"Enlighten the darkness of my heart." This was the persistent request of a person who knew there was an open door right there in front of him, but was still unable to catch a glimpse of the vista it offered because of the obscurity of his own life. And as he "prayed fervently," something like a voice emanated from the painted crucifix and took hold of the attentive and terrified young man, saying:

'Francis, don't you see that my house is crumbling apart? Go, then, and restore it!'

Stunned and trembling, the young man responded, "Yes, Lord, I will do it most willingly."

But he had not understood. He thought that the voice was referring to the church itself which, because it was so old, was threatening to fall into ruins at any moment. "These words filled him with the greatest joy and inner light because in spirit he knew that it was indeed Jesus Christ who had spoken to him" (3 *Comp.* 5:13).

We cannot say for sure what really happened at San Damiano's.

For certain we can say that at San Damiano's Francis had an experience that was spiritually enlightening which opened wide that vast horizon which, up to this point, had been kept hidden, just as the Spoleto valley becomes invisible during November when the fog weighs heavy upon the countryside day in and day out.

It was during this period of time when Francis experienced an upheaval of his spiritual values that he felt the need to travel to Rome on a pilgrimage. The tombs of the apostles Peter and Paul and the seat of the Vicar of Christ on earth were always a magnetic pole attracting the religious fervor of the Middle Ages. And it was no different with Francis. His conversion led him to Rome. We shall see how many other crucial moments of his life took place in Rome.

He went there as the son of a rich merchant. He had bags filled with the best clothes and probably also had a horse with a finely embroidered saddle blanket. He dismounted outside the church of St. Peter's (Bernini's colonnade was not yet in existence, neither had the church's facade by Maderno nor the dome by Michaelangelo been built).

But the poor were there in great numbers. Those whose poverty was authentic and those who faked their misfortune gathered to beg before the gates of the great basilica where the people generally entered and exited with hearts filled with goodness, inclined toward doing good deeds, and expressing their need, each one in his own way, for the mercy of God and the intercession of the Lord's holy apostles. Francis entered the church to venerate the tomb of St. Peter. He begged the first pope to intercede with God for him so that he could understand more clearly what path he ought to take. He stayed there, absorbed in prayer, for a long time before God and in the company of the Blessed Virgin Mary and the holy apostles Peter and Paul. When he came back to the real world, he became aware of an unpleasant sensation that people were being greedy toward God. Or probably it seemed as such to him because of the sound he picked up from the few little coins which the devout people threw piously yet stingily onto St. Peter's tomb. To be honest, it was not up to him to judge the generosity and financial situation of the people who prayed next to him. But we can forgive him his sudden outburst due more to youthful enthusiasm than to negative impressions of others. Francis opened his satchel, took out a big handful of money, and let it roll across the apostle's tomb. Gold and silver coins do not rattle. When they are pitched, they produce a very pleasing and lively sound which everyone recognized right away. At the sound of the money thrown with abandon, the people started to ask themselves who this generous benefactor really was.

Francis was not intimidated by all those curious glances from the people around him. He prayed to the Apostle Peter, he knelt before the Eucharist, and then he headed for the exit.

The pitiable and greedy crowd of poor people who suddenly rushed toward him raised his desires and dreams even more. They touched a whole range of sentiments within him from wanting to be poor like them, at the mercy of good-hearted passers-by and divine providence, to despising the selfish mentality of those who believed that money was the only key which could open the door to happiness. And so, he joined these two contrasting feeling in a single deed of love and scorn: he sold his horse and collected whatever money he still had left and gave it away immediately. Then he decided to change what he had on with the first person he met. He exchanged his rich mantle for an old cheap one. He did the same thing with his tunic and shoes until he had nothing left. He found himself completely in the hands of God for a morsel of bread to eat.

Coming in contact with God started to cost him dearly. He who never before stretched out his hand to beg could now really savor what it meant to be poor. It came clear to him that the sweetness of being poor by far surpassed the blush of feeling ashamed, as had already happened to him when the leper became his brother on the plains of Assisi.

Now he had to return home on foot and in a sorry condition. Peter Bernardone provided him with new clothes and in his worry spoke with his wife about that son of theirs who by now seemed to have gone a bit too far.

But the worst was yet to come. The openness toward God which Francis declared as a result of his experience at San

Damiano's was soon to provoke a clash of ideas that disheartened the young man. He realized there was a gap between the ideals he dreamed of and the chances he had to make them come true. And this gap was bigger than he had figured when all this began.

When Francis returned to visit the little church of San Damiano, the words of Christ re-enkindled, with their utter frankness, the fire burning within: "Francis, do you not see that my house is falling into ruin. Go, then, and rebuild it!"

Francis thought about the repairs. He had to find a way that was simple and that he could do. So, he decided to offer some money. He, who before his conversion used to satisfy many of his desires – from fine dining to extravagant armor – with his father's money, now came up with the unfortunate idea of selling off a bolt of cloth and even his horse at the marketplace in Foligno. This was his way of restoring the church of San Damiano.

He went, in fact, to take the profits of the sale to the priest. But the priest, figuring how these sorts of things came about, wanted no part of it. He must have been quite a clever clergyman. The young, enthusiastic Francis did not like the rebuff he received; he was only repeating the gesture he made at St. Peter's in Rome. There was a small window in the priest's house which was connected to the church. So Francis flung some money into the church through that window. It was up to the priest, then, to decided what to do with it. And with that, he left.

At this point Peter Bernardone weighed the whole situation. He came to the conclusion that his money was absolutely useless in trying to keep his son within the ranks of the merchants or knights. So, he decided to take some drastic measures to resolve the issue at hand. The money to rebuild San Damiano's would not give his son back to him nor would it reap any financial benefit at all. So, he recovered the money, and then he decided to put pressure on his son.

Convinced of the indisputable power of money, he tried to blackmail him first by depriving him of his liberty and then by requiring him to give back all the valuable things he still had. Probably, like many other fathers nowadays, he figured his son was just dabbling around with being poor and could afford to challenge the system precisely because he had lots of money. So, in order to take away all the goods that he had and to pull the rug from under him, the father initiated legal proceedings.

In those days there were two different court systems. Francis rejected the competence of the civil courts by seeking out the protection of the bishop who perhaps had already manifested some sympathy for his case. So his father went to the bishop, Guido II, for judgment in this case. The trial between father and son before the bishop must have been quite a colorful spectacle. Curiosity and gossip spread fast in the small provincial town of Assisi, where any event was a good way to break the monotony of daily living.

The first generation of biographers recounted that Francis made a spectacular gesture on this occasion, one of those kinds of things which he was in the habit of doing:

"In the presence of the bishop he was glad to give his father the money and even the clothes he was wearing. So he stood there completely naked. The bishop then embraced him and covered him with his own mantle" (*Anonymous Perugian* 1:8).

The scene was a very impressive one. Giotto, in one of the frescoes which depicted the series of events in the life of this famous Assisian in the basilica of St. Francis, portrayed this episode with particular intensity. In this fresco, between, the group gathered around Francis and the bishop and, the group centered around the figure of Peter Bernardone, Giotto threw a chasm of deep blue paint to highlight the distance separating them, not just in a physical sense, but also in a spiritual and ideological way as well. There existed a chasm of incomprehension between two different worlds which, from that time on, would be destined to remain apart, even though Francis, in a gesture filled with meaningful symbolism, joined his hands and then stretched out his arms as if to create some sort of bridge between the anguish of his own heart and the pain and hardness of his father.

The painting of Giotto gives vivid testimony to the impact left by such unusual behavior, and it makes us think about the meaning which the Franciscan world soon attached to this irreversible choice. Most certainly Francis accompanied this sensational gesture with some powerful words. *The Legend of the Three Companions* is one of the biographies that relates these words, even though they are not quoted in any of the texts allegedly published before. This fact causes a person to consider whether, during the years following the event, the way the story was transmitted and the flair for making an effect may have played an important role in coloring the facts. Nonetheless, the words handed down to us cannot be far from the truth. Renouncing everything and taking off all the clothes he was wearing was already a very clear indication of what he was up to; the words only added a bit. And so, according to the *Three Companions*, Francis expressed himself in this way: "Listen, all of you, and mark my words. Hitherto I have called Peter Bernardone my father; but because I am resolved to serve God I return to him the money on account of which he was so perturbed, and also the clothes I wore which are his; and from now on I will say 'Our Father who art in heaven,' and not 'my father Peter Bernardone'" (3 *Comp.* 6:20).

I do not think that these words are to be taken as cold and detached as they might seem on first hearing. I believe that Francis was in tears when he uttered them. And they were probably his very own words. I imagine that Peter Bernardone, Madonna Pica, and even the bishop were crying as well.

Meanwhile, Francis set off from Assisi in the direction of the neighboring town of Gubbio. His heart was full of joy and sorrow at the same time.

Francis took advantage of his newly acquired freedom to chant the praises of God and to sing in French in order to see whether he could unchain his tongue, after getting rid of his father's chains. His efforts at freedom were aimed at giving an additional dimension to his individuality. Freedom was not just some unattainable pipe dream nor was it an absolute like that freedom which comes from God.

Francis was free to sing the praises of God and to express his own happiness. He would sing in French, as we do when we make up a song with non-existing words in order to capture a certain mood which we cannot quite define but feel so deeply on the inside.

"Robbers suddenly rushed out upon him. When they asked him in a ferocious tone who he was, the man of God replied confidently in a loud voice, 'I am the herald of the great King. What is that to you?' But they struck him and cast him into a ditch filled with deep snow, saying, 'Lie there, foolish herald of God!'" (1 *Cel.* 16).

This incident happened near Caprignone. Francis' freedom was beginning to take a more defined shape. Freedom meant not only to be without chains; it also meant having the capacity not to hate anyone.

"But he rolled himself about and shook off the snow; and when they had gone away, he jumped out of the ditch and, with great joy, he began to call out the praises of God in a loud voice throughout the grove." Of course, he started to sing in French.

"At length, coming to a certain cloister of monks [the ab-

33

bey of San Verecondo, today called Vallingegno, set between Perugia and Gubbio], he spent several days there as a kitchen helper, wearing a ragged shirt and being satisfied to be filled only with broth. But when all pity was withdrawn from him and he could not even get an old garment, he left the place, not moved by anger, but forced by necessity and he went to the city of Gubbio, where he obtained a small tunic from a certain man who once had been his friend. Then, after some time had elapsed, when the fame of the man of God was beginning to grow and his name was spread among the people, the prior of the aforementioned monastery repented and realized how the man of God had been treated and he came to him and begged pardon for himself and for his monks out of reverence for the Savior" (1 *Cel.* 16).

This is the first time we come across a Benedictine monastery. It seems unfair to look at it in this less-than-favorable light. So, we have to say that the whole story which comes after this speaks positively about that Benedictine world which loved Francis and the Franciscans in a special way. It is not out of place, then, to relate the following example as a way of showing the subsequent affection shown to Francis by the very monastery where is found so little understanding:

"[...]several times the poor and blessed Francis asked for hospitality at the monastery of San Verecondo. The abbot and the monks welcomed him with great delicacy and devotion. This was the place where the miracle of the sow, guilty of devouring a lamb, had happened.

"Not very far from this monastery, blessed Francis had called a chapter of the first three hundred friars. On that occasion the abbot and the monks provided them generously with all they would need according to their possibilities: they gave them barley bread, wheat bread, corn bread, millet bread in abundance; clear drinking water and watered-down cider for the weakest; broad beans and vegetables in large amounts.

This is what the old priest Andrea, who was actually there, passed on to us" (from "*The Story of San Verecondo*").

With his poverty, Francis turned again to his love for lepers. Now he had no more obstacles and could start to live among them.

"Then the holy lover of complete humility went to the lepers and lived with them, serving them most diligently for God's sake; and washing all foulness from them, he wiped away also the corruption of the ulcers, just as he said in his Testament: 'When I was in sins, it seemed extremely bitter to me to look at lepers, and the Lord himself led me among them and I practiced mercy with them'" (1 *Cel.* 17).

Francis, however, in the same Testament quoted by Thomas of Celano, went on to affirm that, in connection with those lepers, what seemed at first to be so bitter became sweet for him, both in regard to his soul as well as his body. This is the reversal of what commonly happens. This is also freedom.

As we have seen, Francis did not have a specific theory on freedom. He acted in his everyday world and he lived his own experiences, and these experiences reflect the brightness of the freedom shining within his soul. This freedom came to light even when he started to restore the church of San Damiano which he had not been able to rebuild with his father's money:

"Then he started back to the city where he began to praise God loudly in the streets and public places; and when he had finished his song of praise, he set to begging for stones with which to restore the church. He called to those passing by: 'Whoever gives me one stone will have one reward; two stones, two rewards; three stones, a treble reward'" (3 *Comp.* 7:21).

He repaired the church of San Damiano with his own hands, and the people of Assisi helped him.

Meanwhile, there persisted both the desire to take action and also the uncertainty as to what to do concretely. This is the reason why he did not waste any time, while he was waiting for God to make his will known to him in a clearer form. After he finished restoring San Damiano's, he started on another church, one near the town walls. Perhaps this was the little church known as "St. Peter's of the Thorn." And when he completed the second one, he did a third. This time it was down in the valley in the middle of a forest. It was an ancient church dedicated to the Blessed Virgin Mary. It was a tiny place, virtually abandoned and neglected.

"When the holy man of God saw how it was thus in ruins, he was moved to pity, because he burned with devotion toward the mother of all good; and he began to live there in great zeal. It was the third year of his conversion when he began to repair this church. At this time he wore a kind of hermit's dress, with a leather girdle about his waist; be carried a staff in his hands and wore shoes on his feet" (1 *Cel*. 21).

The restoration of the three churches took place between the summer of 1207 and the first days of February of 1209.

The third church, dedicated to the Blessed Virgin Mary, was called the Porziuncula or "Little Portion." It is a name we will have to remember quite frequently.

A COMMUNITY IS BORN

Francis was not the type of person who was suited to be by himself. The hermit's life, which he had felt attracted to at first, soon proved to be insufficient for making him happy. He grew up amid the liveliness of a medieval city and right in the middle of the activity in a busy shop. For this reason he was ill suited for the solitude which is found among hermits. The city of Assisi, even though it was restricted in size by its walls and had only a small rural area around it, was always a very attractive place to be because of its politicians and bishops, its artisans and nobles, its small surrounding villages and its mansions within, and also its tradition of enacting legislation in the public square. Francis was born in a city such as this, and this was the place he felt he belonged. We can say that Francis' human make-up was situated within the kind of life associated with all the activities of a city.

This is why his first attempt to lead a hermit's life did not produce any concrete results. During his lifetime the saint spent many periods of time in a hermitage. But these occasional events were only parenthetical episodes which lasted just long enough to help him get over a bout with spiritual fatigue. But the fact that he realized that the hermit's life was not right for him did not mean that he had overcome all of his doubts. He knew well what he should not do; he just was not sure what he was supposed to do.

Meanwhile, he still had to go begging for food from door to door, though he felt so terribly embarrassed to do so. He sought help and he asked for stones to repair the churches. He stayed among the lepers, but became less and less identified with the life of a hermit, even though he carried around the external signs of this lifestyle, namely the type of garb he wore and the walking stick he used.

One day Francis participated in the celebration of the Mass at St. Mary's of the Porziuncula. It was the feast of St. Matthias the apostle. According to the common agreement of historians, this was February 24, 1209.

On that day the passage of the Gospel which was read was taken from Matthew, chapter ten, or Luke, chapter nine. It was the passage where Christ indicated to his apostles what form of life they ought to follow if they wanted to consider themselves his disciples.

"As you go," admonishes Jesus in the Gospel of Matthew, "make this announcement: 'The reign of God is at hand!' Cure the sick, raise the dead, heal the lepers, expel demons. The gift you have received, give as a gift. Provide yourselves with neither gold nor silver nor copper in your belts; no traveling bag, no change of shirt, no sandals, no walking staff" (10:7-10, NAB). This extract from the Gospel immediately brought about in him an intuition or insight. At last he understood what he was to do.

According to his first biographers, Francis blurted out the following exclamation: "This is what I wish! This is what I want! This is what I long to do with all my heart!"

Francis threw away everything he did not really need. Above all, he got rid of all the vestiges of the eremitical life and refused to wear the hermit's garb. Instead he put on what the Gospel said he was to wear: a tunic and a rope instead of a belt to keep the tunic closefitting around his waist.

There is something very characteristic about Francis' behavior: he did not need a whole lot of time to come to a decision between the time he heard the Gospel and the time he put it into practice. As soon as a particular teaching became clear to him, he knew right away how to give it a practical application without spending a lot of time meditating on it or writing a book about it. He was truly a very intuitive person. He applied the Gospel word for word, even in the smallest detail, because in it he saw the Son of God.

There is no document left that testifies to the fact that Francis went out looking for some followers after he heard the Gospel in the Porziuncula. He did not have the foggiest idea nor the faintest intention to start a community of his own. Like many other things in his life, the group of followers eventually came about rather unexpectedly and without any coaxing. Once more, reality and experience came before theory. This is how it all came about.

The life of the young man who went around restoring churches became the talk of the town in Assisi. Inevitably there was that typical mockery and criticism which give small towns their particular flavor.

Some of the people of Assisi, however, looked upon him as possibly a messenger from God. And, since he was poor and preached poverty, the first person who felt deeply moved by him was a rich man. His name was Bernard of Quintavalle. Bernard was the type of person who was sensitive to the voice of his own conscience but at the same time was very practical. Francis' life made him uneasy, but he wanted to study him more closely before he came to any conclusions about him. So, out of admiration and friendship, he invited him to his house, the exterior of which we can still see today on the street in Assisi which is named after him: "Bernard of Quintavalle Street." This was one of the wealthier, better appointed homes of Assisi. Perhaps it was not anything exceptional, but it had such a supply of grain and wine that in those days it was enough to guarantee a high standard of living.

Bernard invited Francis to his house several times. Finally he was convinced that the son of Peter Bernardone was neither a lunatic nor a cheat. One night, in fact, he witnessed Francis at prayer. Perhaps it was by accident, perhaps on purpose. When a person is really praying, he or she cannot be deceptive; and a feigned prayer is far too theatrical. For this reason Bernard was convinced of Francis' holiness. Someone who is crazy or someone who is faking it could not have prayed the way he did.

In the morning Bernard stood before Francis and said to him: "Brother, it is my intention to follow you in your way of life." Bernard was aware that he was in for some folly. But that folly of Francis was something that both turned him off and also pleased him very much. It was worth giving it a try.

After Bernard, came Peter Catanii. He was not as rich as Bernard; but what he had going for him was that he was an expert in law and also a canon of the cathedral.

Now the three of them formed a group. And a group has its own existence which is not just the same thing as duplicating or triplicating what a single person would do by oneself. So, they decided to make a go at a practical way of living together. Taking into consideration the kind of fellow Francis was, it was obvious that he would have recourse to the Gospel as the go-between when the three of them set out to encounter God.

"They headed toward a church in the city, and upon entering it they would kneel down and pray, 'Lord God, Father of glory, we ask you in your mercy to reveal to us what we have to do. 'When they finished praying, they asked the priest of that same church, who was present there, 'Sir, please show us the Gospel of our Lord Jesus Christ.' After the priest opened the book, since they were not experts in letters, they right away found the passage which said, 'if you would be perfect, sell everything you have, give it to the poor and thus you will have treasure in heaven.' Turning to another page they read, 'if you wish to come after me, deny yourselves, take up your cross, and follow me.' Once again, they found another pericope, 'Take nothing with you on your journey, neither walking stick nor traveling bag; no bread, no money; no one is to have two tunics'" (*Anonymous Perugian* 2:10-11).

These passages were, respectively, Mt 19-21 and 16:24 and Lk 9:3.

So Bernard decided to sell all he had (and it was quite a bit) and Peter disposed of his few belongings, and they distributed the money to the poor in the public square. At that moment both Bernard and Peter reached the point of no return. Their choice was irreversible.

After selling everything, they did not even own a house. They found themselves free, but also without a roof over their heads. So, they went down the hill to St. Mary's of the Porziuncula and there, a short distance from the little church, they settled into an old, abandoned Benedictine house that was falling apart; or else they used some logs and branches to fashion some sort of a hut. Here they spent their first night of poverty.

Another man named Giles joined them at the Porziuncula. And then there were four.

Giles was a farmer. Together with his brothers he made his living from the earth, tending to the fields. He also had heard the talk about Francis and had watched those three strange men living in the valley. Very quickly he stopped believing in all the gossip and started to be convinced that he was being called to join them. So he went.

Now there were the four of them: a merchant, a noble-man, a canon, and a farmer. At this point it is interesting to note what happened in regard to the events that brought to light Francis' plan for building a community, a plan which many people soon forgot – perhaps even the saint himself – when his followers numbered in the thousands and quantity became more important than quality.

No sooner had they gathered together as a foursome that there emerged a common conviction: it was not enough to preach and give good example to the citizens of Assisi. They had to carry their message much farther. They had to reach out to people with whom they had not yet come into contact. So the four of them made up two groups. Francis and Giles went to the Marches of Ancona (quite a trip in those days!). Bernard and Peter headed in the direction of Tuscany.

They were not going there to preach. They simply went to carry a message to all the people about their existence and about the joy they felt.

They did not have any special purpose to their journey, as we might think of doing these days, like doing apostolic work or making converts. They took off like swallows in the spring, urged on by an inner impulse to give testimony to the joy which welled up in their hearts as a result of the new way of living they had discovered.

Francis sang out in French, praising and blessing the Lord with a loud and clear voice, and he urged the people to fear and love God and to turn away from their sins. Giles limited himself to the comment: "What he says is right! Believe him!"

The story related here is taken from the *Anonymous Perugian* (3:15), which drew its material from the *Legend of the Three Companions*. None of the other early biographers re-count this first venturing forth of the band of four. Moreover, in the texts mentioned above, what appears as an excuse for a failed preaching mission actually, with hindsight, turns out to be Francis' "prophecy" regarding how he anticipated the great expansion of the Order.

During the course of the year 1209 the group grew and very soon they numbered eight. And more and more often they were sent forth from the Porziuncula in the direction of the Marches, of the Rieti Valley, of Tuscany. When they reached the villages and towns, the people noticed how different they were – in their style of clothing and by the way they lived – from all the other religious they had come to know. Moreover, they came across as something out of the wild. Hence it was quite natural that they aroused people's interest and generated a lot of enthusiasm, gossip, and sarcasm. Their simple antics mushroomed into adventures of the imagination and became the subject matter for future story-telling to edify and astonish the folks who listened.

Every once in a while, someone who was more cultured or who paid some attention to them would ask them what Order they belonged to. This question found the followers of Francis unprepared to come up with a response. They just did not know what to answer. Sometimes they simply introduced themselves by saying, "We are the penitents who come from Assisi."

From their huts surrounding the Porziuncula they left on their missionary journeys, and to them they came back. The instances of departure and regathering tended to form a rhythmical pattern.

In late 1209 Francis' group was a very novel one and, probably, a particularly successful one from a psychological point of view. What constituted their originality? We shall try to put our finger on it by focusing attention not only on the year 1209 but also on the following years which provide us with many of the necessary experiences. The life of the group was based on certain insights gleaned from the Gospel: a poor life, on the road, together with the brothers. This gospel project which had loomed large in the mind of the man from Assisi became explicitly concrete just like an almost literal replay of the model Jesus proposed to his disciples. The apostles, in fact, went out two by two to announce that the reign of God was near without giving anything specific about it. The way a person needed to prepare for this reign was through a change of heart, a conversion. All this was communicated to everyone free of charge and in poverty.

After every journey everyone would come together to share his own experiences in the apostolate and to relate the miracles that had happened during a gathering in a prayerful setting which Jesus had set up for them. Jesus brought them together to pray with each other and to teach them and thereby to verify their actual experiences. This is the model of community which is found in the Gospel. We read it in St. Luke's text which could very well be the version which Francis heard at the Porziuncula when he began his new style of living:

"Jesus now called the Twelve together and gave them power and authority to overcome all demons and to cure diseases. He sent them forth to proclaim the reign of God and heal the afflicted. Jesus advised them: 'Take nothing for the journey, neither walking staff nor traveling bag; no bread, no money. No one is to have two coats. Stay at whatever house you enter and proceed from there. When people will not receive you, leave that town and shake its dust from your feet as a testimony against them.' So they set out and went from village to village, spreading the good news everywhere and curing diseases. ... The apostles on their return related to Jesus all they had accomplished. Taking them with him, he retired to a town called Bethsaida" (Lk 9:1-6,10).

Now that we have explained the model itself as given in the Gospel, we can see how Francis translated it into his own situation.

The friars went out two by two to witness to a new way of life and to speak about the Reign of God and about conversion, just like the apostles, without any complicated theological issues. In other words, Francis and his companions wanted to create a disposition, an atmosphere for being open to experiencing God.

After their apostolic journey, the friars returned to the Porziuncula; they told stories about the marvelous works which God had accomplished, and they entered into a time of prayer and study. If any of the readers know anything in depth about the Franciscan world, they would already be able to account for the source from which Francis drew his inspiration for his type of apostolic expression and for his style of pulling away for quiet time and of celebrating chapters.

Only in broad strokes have we described what life was like at St. Mary's of the Porziuncula. It was a way of living styled directly on the example of the Gospel. But really we did not give any of the particulars. Now is the time to do that.

The apostles, after traveling through cities and villages, returned to come together among themselves around the person of Jesus. Francis copied this point of the Gospel but adapted it to his present situation with an original interpretation.

Once they had carried out their mission, the friars began to meet again, to come together, and to rejuvenate themselves spiritually and psychologically. It is clear that during the span of a year they did not spend all their time together. Francis was grounded in the Gospel, and he was endowed with such an unusual psychological insight that he stood above many of his learned contemporaries. He understood the human condition very well. This is why he was convinced that his friars should never live like monks enclosed within the four walls of a monastery. He knew that every person had to have his own space to live in, but he did not want it to be carved out of a structure, like a house. Rather, the group centered around a discourse or a teaching, not around a place.

Several times a year the friars would gather around St. Mary's of the Porziuncula, and this encounter would come to be called a "chapter." This is the same name that the monks living in monasteries gave to their regular meetings. The difference for Francis, however, was that his cloister and his cell were the mountains and hills all around and the sky above.

The most famous of these chapters in the history of Franciscanism was the one called the "Chapter of Mats" which brought together, it seems, about 5,000 friars.

What did they do at this chapter? It is important to find this out because it was the primary experience among the companions of the Assisi Penitents that helped them feel like a real family. After their pilgrimages for work and preaching and prayer, the brothers came together. They had so many things to relate: the marvels of God which were at work as they carried on their activities; the experience they had; the knowledge they gained; the most effective methods for bringing people closer to God; the ways that worked well for preaching about love and for growing in love. They listened attentively to one another in order to treasure each other's experiences and to enrich their basic desire to get to know one another deeply.

When I read the book of the *Fioretti*, I have the impression of actually participating in this chapter.

Listening to the friars telling stories and sharing their opinions, I feel as though I am really right there with them as they build up community and together give praise to God. The *Fioretti* are one story after another, providing eyewitness accounts; for example:

"How, because of an evil thought Francis had against

Brother Bernard, he commanded him to step three times with his feet on his throat and mouth" (*Fior.* 3).

"How St. Francis observed Lent on an island in a lake near Perugia, fasting forty days and forty nights and not eating anything except a piece of bread" (*Fior.* 7).

"How, as they traveled along the road, Francis taught Brother Leo about those things which constitute perfect joy" (*Fior.* 8).

"How St. Francis freed some turtle doves and made nests for them" (*Fior.* 22).

"How Brother Masseo learned from Christ the virtue of holy humility" (*Fior.* 32).

"How St. Anthony of Padua, the Friar Minor, preached marvelously to a consistory of cardinals" (*Fior.* 39).

Everything was done "for the glory of Christ Jesus. Amen!"

The chapters served these purposes: to get to know others and to get oneself known by others; to discover God's plan and to understand one's own mission in life; to find the best way to move forward. In these chapters there grew a wealth of experience, leadership with enthusiasm, and the serenity of prayer.

TAKING THE GOSPEL SERIOUSLY

When, at St. Mary's of the Porziuncula on that memorable 24th of February, Francis decided to adhere literally to the passage of the Gospel he heard during Mass on the feast of the apostle St. Matthias, he did not just make a symbolic gesture. He put aside the walking stick of the hermit, and by the same token he deliberately chose not to follow the current spirituality. He took off his shoes, and thereby highlighted his complete availability to be free from the world. He did away with the leather belt around his waist that held the money bag, and in doing so he demonstrated his complete trust in Divine Providence which never abandons those who put their total confidence in God. But he did not do all this flippantly. It was not just the impulse of youthful enthusiasm.

In fact, before taking this action, he waited for the priest until the end of the Eucharistic celebration and asked him if he might be willing to explain in detail the meaning of the gospel passage. He was fully aware of what he was going to do and he came to terms with the fact that it involved some essential turns on the road of life. For this reason he did not want to rely only on his own understanding; so he turned to someone who, in the name of the Church, could give him some good advice. All of this points to the fact that Francis was not naive nor was he easily prone to be swept away with unbridled enthusiasm. The months of quiet prayer and the habits he had developed for considering those things which pertained to God convinced Francis that the word of Christ was the only one in which he would place his confidence and for which he would consider it worthwhile spending his life.

For Francis the Gospel had to be taken seriously.

We also think, as many others do, that we are taking the Gospel seriously. But there is a big difference. For us the Gospel is a point of reference, a goal toward which we strive with sacrifice and much effort as we give up the delights of the flesh and the world. It was not that way, however, with Francis. He discovered that the Gospel was not so much a point of arrival, but rather a starting point from which he could begin to construct in freedom the wonder-filled canvas of life.

When he, for the first time, approached the leper as a brother, he had a unique experience which he had never thought about before. In fact, he talks about this at the beginning of his Testament: "When I had once become acquainted with them, what had previously nauseated me became a source of spiritual and physical consolation for me."

The experience of the leper turned all of his usual points of reference upside down. He set out to accomplish a heroic act of self-sacrifice, but instead ended up having a most pleasing experience. The bitterness was transformed into sweetness not only in his mind (which of course would be understandable in someone with an ascetic bent), but even in his very body.

That encounter toppled his whole approach to spirituality which saw his following of the Gospel as "sacrifice to gain heaven." Instead, the Gospel could also be something beautiful, enjoyable and pleasant. Francis had discovered the gist of the Gospel which made it achievable and livable and acceptable not only as an ascetic practice (that is, as the sacrifice response to gain heaven), but also as the consequence of taking on as one's own and of appreciating the values which Christ himself presented. Moreover, the Gospel becomes joyful and Christianity becomes a joyous and appetizing experience. It is a gift to be offered to one's brothers and sisters. It is a discovery on which to build a whole life.

So, Francis had a message for everybody. He believed that, by following the Gospel, he had the key for the solution of the world's problems. He made practical a new way of life and offered to the world an example of this life by means of the experience of his own group of companions, just like a good host who offers his guests a taste of his own wine.

In this way Francis and his companions journeyed about; they accomplished their work and came together again as common people but with a new inspiration that gave a whole different meaning to what they did, no matter how normal it seemed from its appearance. To others he said by word and deed: "Brother, Sister, I have confidence in you! I am looking for those fine qualities you have received from God as a gift. My Brother, my Sister, shall we list them?" And Francis would enumerate them so positively:

Where there is Love and Wisdom
there is neither Fear nor Ignorance.
Where there is Patience and Humility,
there is neither Anger nor Annoyance.
Where there is Poverty and Joy,
there is neither Cupidity nor Avarice.
Where there is Peace and Contemplation,
there is neither Care nor Restlessness.
Where there is the Fear of God to guard the dwelling,
here no enemy can enter.

Where there is Mercy and Prudence,
there is neither Excess nor Harshness (*Adm.* XXVII).

Think positively, and you will see how quickly your negative thoughts disappear; they will not even take root.

This is what Francis believed because it was the Gospel. The good reality is a thousand times superior to the bad, and it is foolish to base oneself on a reality that is contrary to gospel values. For this reason he was the bearer of a reality that was seen to be both revolutionized and revolutionary. I did not say "a revolutionary thinker" because Francis was no philosopher. His biographers are in agreement that the saint made a very strong impact upon the people he came in contact with. They were the nobility and the ordinary folk, the clergy and the laity, the cardinals and the farmers, the rich and the beggars. In order to bring together the many testimonials which pertain to Francis, we decided to use the book of the Fioretti which, even though it lacks a lot of historical accuracy, it still communicates the spiritual and psychological truth of the matter. Chapter ten of the *Fioretti* says that, while Francis was staying at St. Mary's of the Porziuncula, Brother Masseo of Marignano made the remark to him when he returned from the woods where he had been praying:

"'Why after you? Why after you? Why after you?' St. Francis replied: 'What do you mean, Brother Masseo?' 'I mean, why does all the world seem to be running after you, and everyone seems to want to see you and hear you and obey you? You are not a handsome man. You do not have great learning or wisdom. You are not a nobleman. So why is all the world running after you?'" (*Fior.* 10).

Francis was glad to hear Masseo talk in this way and he punctuated his answer with great clarity: because God had chosen him "to do this marvelous work which he intended him to do."

This "marvelous work" was nothing other than the repetition of that first adventure which Christ himself presented to the world through the challenge of the apostles. It was not an accident that the example of the apostles' life became the identifying mark for unfolding the plans of this man from Assisi.

The challenge of gospel living is meant to shed light on the whole world and not to be enclosed in the tiny space of some hermitage or convent that is inattentive to the person who knocks at the door.

REPORTS ABOUT FRANCIS' EXPERIENCE

St. Francis did not have a recruiting office, nor did he go among the people looking for someone to follow him.

When somebody arrived at St. Mary's of the Porziuncula to ask if he could stay there as a friar, Francis welcomed him, like an unexpected pleasure. It goes without saying that every new presence was also a new problem. But the man of God resolved the problems one by one as they occurred, and little by little the whole situation became more solidified in the process. Furthermore, his own spirituality and that of his group grew in the same way. So, after the first apostolic journey, Sabbatino, Morico, and John of Cappella joined Bernard, Peter Catanii, and Giles. The new ones arrived at the Porziuncula from Assisi just a few days after the others had returned from their missionary efforts. The three new recruits came to their decision between the spring and the summer of 1209, and now they brought the fruit of their discernment to Francis. Before they would give up everything they had and turn it over to the poor, they would have to become poor themselves, each in his own time.

To learn to be poor is very wearisome, but from a spiritual point of view it has immeasurable benefits. A person who becomes poor by choice takes on a similarity to Christ even during one's earthly journey through life, becomes a sign of humility, support, friendship, and really makes sense out of the Providence of God. For this reason the Lord calls someone "blessed" who goes out of one's way to capture the real meaning of voluntary poverty, while condemning to the eternal fires someone who puts constraints upon the friars not to have anything in this world.

Even though poverty has much value from the perspective of spirituality, it is a whole other thing when looking for supplies. The growing number of men was placing quite a burden upon the group: in order to eat they really needed some bread! And in the 13th century you did not just find bread in the garbage cans, much less meat. To look for bread for six or twelve people you would have to search all day and hopefully, from time to time, you would come across a little something to go with it, and maybe a glass of wine. But it was not easy.

These men, more or less from the well-to-do class, now had to compete with town beggars just to get something to eat. And they were not successful in finding work. They could not even earn a living. Begging was so hard. Going like that from door to door, knocking at the door of the citizens who were their well-off former companions and neighbors, made them feel like dogs who had just been given a beating. Every now and then they skipped a door when the memories were too painful or the taunting of the local inhabitants was too sarcastic.

In Assisi the problem with food, among other things, was provoking a hornet's nest of gossip and criticism. Those who were always poor now had to compete with new unforeseen rivals. Those who were related to the new beggars were embarrassed and were suspect of any future question that they might have to shoulder the burden of these fellows who seemed to live dissolute lives. Those who were accustomed to be superficial were glad to find something novel and stimulating to talk about. Among all of these, including the group of people who were touched by all these events and pondered them in their hearts, there was a lot of indecisiveness regarding what all these events happening before their very eyes really meant.

Somebody who highly resented the beggars, said: "What! You have thrown away your own possessions, and now you want to eat at the expense of others" (cf. 3 *Comp*. 9:35).

The shame of begging was like a blanket of fog in the middle of a sunny day. And feeling heavily burdened, it cast a cold pall over the men. This was so even when they had enough bread to eat. Francis felt the pain of all this more intensely than the others. He had a special sensitivity to people's social status, and that sensitivity made him the butt of jokes because of his dangerous longing for knighthood and for a title of nobility.

This resulted in his personally taking upon himself extraordinary humiliations for the sake of sparing his companions. In spite of this it still was neither possible, nor was it right, to accomplish everything. Records testify that he tried to upgrade the dignity of their sacrifice of going out for alms; in fact, he thought in his heart that in exalting humiliation to an heroic level he could easily convince the eager minds of his companions that they were fulfilling a chivalrous impulse. This was basic psychology, but it produced some noble, though momentary, effects. Still it is worth noting that, since he talked so much about this topic (as his biographers indicate), perhaps he was hiding a deep inner revulsion to begging which caused him much grief and suffering.

In those early days there was no danger that someone would get used to begging. But in case this would become a problem along with the other negative things they encountered (and this did happen when there were quite a number of friars), Francis made it very clear that alms were only the last resort to fill up what was lacking in the fruits of their labor, and that only when they were preaching could they consider it to be a well furnished table prepared by the Lord for his apostles. First comes work – he said in the Rule – and if the friars are not paid for their labors, only then do they have recourse to the "table of the Lord" which, in such a case, they ought to seek out without any embarrassment whatsoever. "I work with my own hands and I am still determined to work; and with all my heart I want all the other friars to be busy with some kind of work that can be carried out without scandal. Those who do not know how to work should learn," he said in his Testament. This leads us to understand that among his followers there must have been some who knew nothing of physical labor because they were born into nobility or became knights.

On one occasion, the unrelenting burden of begging for alms spurred Francis on to pour out his heart to Bishop Guido. The bishop had a lot of good sense and knew from experience the ways of the world.

"Why don't you accept some donations or at least hold on to some of the possessions of your followers," he counseled. Already he could picture a new monastery, powerful and lively, prospering in the ambience of the diocese.

But he was wrong!

"My Lord", replied Francis, "if we have possessions, then we will need arms to protect them because it is from property that arises quarrels and strife. And in such a way the love of God and neighbor is blocked. For this reason we have decided to possess nothing" (*Anonymous Perugian*, 3:17).

In speaking thus Francis provided a rationale for their poverty and at the same time outlined a remedy against conflicts and wars, namely, no ownership.

Taking into consideration how things went in the society of

his day, Francis was of the opinion that it was not possible to live according to the Gospel if a person was loaded down with house or lands. And since he did not know a half-way point between possessions and alms, he thought he had to pay a penalty for his ideal. So he continued to turn to the charity of others and enjoined his companions to do the same when it was necessary. Still, because of his innate refinement of spirit, he figured that he could reduce the severity of the problem if he cast the whole situation into an ascetic or romantic light.

One day, and this happened quite a bit later when Brother Masseo was already part of the group, "he, taking Brother Masseo as his companion, set out on the road toward the Province of France. And one day when they came to a village and they were quite hungry, they went begging for bread for the love of God, according to the Rule. And St. Francis went along one street and Brother Masseo along another." It happened that Francis scavenged a nice little piece of bread, while Masseo, who was more good-looking and congenial, brought back even a whole loaf of bread. The Saint was so happy and said excitedly: "Oh Brother Masseo, we do not deserve such a great treasure as this!" He repeated these words several times. Brother Masseo responded: "Dear Father, how can this be called a treasure when there is such poverty and such a lack of things that are necessary? For here we have no cloth, no knife, no dish, no bowl, no house, no table, no waiter, no waitress." St. Francis answered: "This is what I consider a great treasure – where nothing has been prepared by human labor. But everything here has been supplied by Divine Providence, as is evident in the begged bread, the fine stone table, and the clear spring" (*Fior.* 13).

In those days there was no pollution, and the bread baked in the wood ovens was really quite good.

When Philip the Tall joined the group at the Porziuncula, the number came to eight. Out in the fields around the place there was a bit of work during the day. The woods took on a reddish color, and the mist made its way over the land. This meant that there were opportunities for work. It was the right time to sow seed and to pick the olives. The farmers needed every available hand in exchange for a bowl of soup and a handful of vegetables to take home.

When the work in the fields was over and the world began to shiver and the people retired to their homes to take shelter against the cold of winter, the eight felt the need to set out to evangelize beyond the confines of the city of Assisi. Winter was not the best time to leave on a preaching excursion; nonetheless, in winter people were more free and better disposed to listen, especially in those villages and castles where farming and simple handicrafts – now restricted by the bad weather and the lack of sunlight – constituted the major part of the people's work. Going forth two by two, as the Lord commanded in the Gospel, the eight divided their world into four parts, in the sign of the cross: Two went north. Two went south. Two went east. Two went west. Francis set off in the direction of Terni, Narni, Poggio Bustone, and Rieti. When they got back to the Porziuncula the winter was not yet over, but it was already the year of grace 1210.

A new follower named Angelo Tancredi accompanied Francis back to Assisi. Angelo was a soldier. Perhaps he had a bit of nobility in him, perhaps not. Nonetheless, whatever his lineage was, people liked to see in him those elements of knightly nobility which were missing in this movement. And so, he was received by the others as a knight. Then came John of St. Constance, Barbaro, and Bernard Vigilante. Now there were twelve. (If we count Francis, there were thirteen). History, however, is not very clear at all when and how these first companions came on the scene.

The return, as always, was a coming back to a grand celebration. At last they gathered back together to recount their many experiences and to tell about all those things which the Lord had done through them in the villages far away. The friars met and talked about the plan of God which was unfolding day after day; they prayed together, and they constituted their own mode of living together and of coping with suffering and of interpreting the reality around them, thus creating a "chapter." This "chapter," made up of real events and happening in real time, actually embodies the heart of their lived experience.

"The strangest thing that ever happened to us" said Sabbatino – "is that wherever we went, the people were amazed to see us. It was probably because of the way we dressed, or maybe because our way of life is so different! Somebody even took us to be some kind of boorish folk who are supposed to live in the forest. Others thought us to be wild men. When, however, we started to talk about God and to give God praise and when we would invite all the people to make peace and not to hate one another because of a problem in the fields or because of a stolen chicken or because of some altercation between parties and when we helped them see that we could be happy with only a simple tunic and one pair of pants and that it was possible to go around barefoot without bearing a grudge again those who wear shoes – even then they took us for lunatics. Some people, though, were impressed by what we said and did; they had a change of heart and wanted to leave everything and follow us."

"You see" – explained Francis – "people who are married with spouse and children at home cannot follow us on our preaching mission. They must not do so, in fact, because God has given them other responsibilities. They, however, can preach penance, like us, but in their own village or castle. They have to change their lives and not be so attached to the riches which they already have. The important thing is not so much to travel around but to live according to the Gospel. Then, ... they also took me for a lunatic! Oh, it was to be expected. People even took the Lord Jesus for a crazy man. Anyone who lives or speaks differently from the other is considered to be crazy, but that really means that the others cannot understand. Then we also had to put up with mockery and nasty jokes. They grabbed us by our capuche and dragged us through the mud and entertained the world at our expense. Don't you think a little suffering is necessary for the love of God?"

"On the other hand, we noticed" – recounted Peter Catanii (who had been a canon of the cathedral at Assisi) – "how good it was to stop in one of those small, quiet, unadorned, and dilapidated churches which nonetheless reserved the Blessed Sacrament. And it was good to stop in front of a crucifix at a crossroads along the way and pray that God would inspire us which way to go, right or left. And we would willingly say the prayer which you taught us, Francis: 'We adore you, o Christ, and we bless you here and in all the churches throughout the whole world because by your holy cross you have redeemed the world' (3 Comp. 37). And when the people would ask us where we came from or what Order we belonged to, we would just say that we are penitents from Assisi."

"We are penitents too" – they responded all together. "What an experience this has been! Truly it has been great to live just as the Gospel says. And we never thought about this before."

"Yes, it was good even when they tore our tunics off and left us there shivering in the cold, wearing only our pants!" added John of Cappella who was a big and hefty specimen of humanity.

"But then they gave us our tunics back and apologized to us for what they did," continued Peter Catanii. And everyone laughed and praised God because they could not imagine Peter, who was the most learned among them, returning with just his pants on.

Bernard then related a beautiful experience – the kind for which one praises God – because it probably indicated how they came upon the right way to make people understand the Gospel.

Here's the story:

"About this time two brothers were searching for lodging throughout the city of Florence but were unable to find any. When they found a house with a porch containing an oven, they said to each other: 'We can stay here.' Therefore they asked the lady of the house if she would please welcome them into her home. She immediately refused. They begged her at least to allow them to spend the night on the porch near the stove.

"She permitted them to do this. However, when her husband came home, and saw the brothers on the porch near the stove, he told her: 'Why did you give lodging to these two rogues?' She answered: 'I did not allow them inside the house but gave them permission to stay on the porch where they could not steal anything from us except the firewood.' On account of this distrust, they refused to give the brothers anything to cover themselves, although the weather was severely cold. During the night the brothers got up for matins and went to the nearest church.

"When morning came, the lady went to church for Mass and saw the brothers devoutly and humbly praying. She said to herself: 'If these men were evil, as my husband claimed, they would not be praying so devoutly.' While she was thinking these things, a man named Guido was going around the church distributing alms to the poor. When he approached the brothers, he attempted to give each one a coin, as he had done to the others, but they refused to take it. He told them: 'Why don't you accept the coins like the other poor? I see that you are poor and needy.' One of the brothers, Bernard, answered: 'Indeed it is true that we are poor, but our poverty is not burdensome for us as for the other poor because we have become poor by the grace of God and in fulfillment of his counsel.' Astonished, Guido asked them if they had possessed anything in the world. They told him that they indeed had, but for the love of God had given them to the poor.

"When the woman saw how the brothers had refused the coins, she approached them and said: 'Christians, if you want to come back with me, I will gladly take you into my home.' The brothers answered her humbly: 'May the Lord reward you.' When Guido saw that the brothers were unable to find lodging, he took them to his own house and told them: 'Look, this is the lodging which the Lord prepared for you. Stay here as long as you want.' But they thanked God for showing them his mercy and hearing the cries of the poor. They stayed with Guido several days. Because of their words and good example, he was afterwards very generous to the poor" (*Anonymous Perugian* 5).

This exchange of their various experiences prompted much reflection, brought them encouragement and support, and opened up for them a new sunny horizon, even though no one labored under any illusion about how rough the road would actually be. Their prayer and their love for each other reinforced their convictions.

There was, moreover, a certain similarity to their experiences. In all of the accounts some common elements are always found: enthusiasm, the initial difficulties which were overcome by the strength of standing up for what they believed, and the openness of the people to accept the new way of living they proposed because they saw how sincere was their motivation.

The *Anonymous Perugian* explains:

"The people could see how serene the brothers were in the face of suffering which they accepted patiently from the Lord, how intent they were in praying with devotion, how they refused to receive or even to hold any money as their own but instead lived in poverty, and how they only desired the good of one another, as a sign that they were disciples of Jesus. As a result, many people were touched to the heart and expressed their sorrow, asking forgiveness for the ways they treated others harshly. The friars forgave them from their hearts, responding with great joy, 'May the Lord forgive you!" (*Anonymous Perugian*, 5:24).

Hence, these first "chapters" (or reunions) after their evangelizing pilgrimages at the Porziuncula became exciting moments for sharing the oneness of their life because they knew everyone was bound together around a common message taught by Christ and around that awesome work which would soon be carried out. In the end, when everybody had the chance to speak and tell his story and after they had prayed and had recommitted themselves to their high intentions, Francis gathered up everything, as if he were collecting breadcrumbs so that they would not fall to the ground and get lost. He brought together the experiences and the proposals of the friars, he filtered them through his own personal perspective, he made them his own, and he incorporated them into his own spiritual journey. By doing this he could conclude the chapter with warm and familial exhortations which even today are preserved in the form of schematic summaries.

Thus did he speak as he stood on the steps of the Virgin's altar:

"St. Paul tells us, 'No one can say Jesus is Lord, except in the Holy Spirit' (1 Cor 12:3) and, 'There is no one who does good, no, not even one (Rom 3:12). And so, when a man envies his brother the good God says or does through him, it is like committing a sin of blasphemy, because he is really envying God. who is the only source of every good" (*Adm*. VIII).

"Our Lord says in the Gospel, 'Love your enemies' (Mt 5:44). A man really loves his enemy when he is not offended by the injury done to himself, but for the love of God feels burning sorrow for the sin his enemy has brought on his own soul, and proves his love in a practical way" (*Adm.* IX).

"We can be sure that a man is a true religious and has the spirit of God if his lower nature does not give way to pride when God accomplishes some good through him, and if he seems all the more worthless and inferior to others in his own eyes. Our lower nature is opposed to every good" (*Adm.* XII).

"Blessed are the peacemakers, for they shall be called children of God' (Mt 5:9). They are truly peacemakers who are able to preserve their peace of mind and heart for love of our Lord Jesus Christ, despite all that they suffer in this world" (*Adm.* XV).

"Blessed that friar who loves his brother as much when he is sick and can be of no use to him as when he is well and can be of use to him. Blessed that friar who loves and respects his brother as much when he is absent as when he is present and who would not say anything behind his back that he could not say charitably to his face" (*Adm.* XXV).

In this atmosphere of encountering one another and pondering what was being said, they gathered together, like the apostles in the Upper Room, around St. Mary's of the Porziuncula.

THE LATERAN THREATENS TO COLLAPSE

The number twelve. There is something special about it. For those people who have made the mission of the apostles their own way of life it holds a special emotional attachment. This, then, is probably the reason why, when the group at the Porziuncula reached this number, the holy man of Assisi began to answer the question, "What are we to do?" The "apostolic college," which we learned from the Acts of the Apostles, was a single-minded group that grew out of the early Church. Something similar was now happening to the group of twelve from the Porziuncula. They felt the need to take on their own identity and character.

Considering what was going on in the Church at that time and realizing the current monastic mind-set that certainly colored his whole outlook, Francis felt something deep within himself and quickly made it known:

"I see, Brothers, that God in his mercy means to increase our company: let us therefore go to our holy Mother the Roman Church and lay before the Supreme Pontiff what our Lord has begun to work through us; so that with his consent and direction we may continue what we have undertaken" (3 *Comp.* 7:46).

So, they decided to head to Rome to see the Supreme

Pontiff. Before they set out, however, they chose a leader for their journey, someone who would set up the schedule and give them the necessary time and space for prayer. The person they chose was Bernard.

Rome in the thirteenth century was not as complicated as it is today. Even though there were no radios nor telephones, the penitents from Assisi right away made contact with Bishop Guido who himself was in Rome at the time. They were happy to meet up with each other, but the bishop quickly came to the conclusion that these holy men could be coming to Rome with the intention of abandoning Assisi. He knew well how the Assisians could gossip, and so it was not difficult for him to imagine that they were running away from all this. He told them very frankly what was on his mind; but, when be came to understand the real reason for their trip, be gave his approval and offered to facilitate their audience with the Pope.

Bishop Guido was not deprived of friends while in Rome. One of them – John Cardinal Colonna of St. Paul, the bishop of Sabina – was a very influential man. During these times the cardinals were few, but they wielded a lot of power. Cardinal John was a holy person and, in Guido's eyes, presenting this solid and enthusiastic group from Assisi to him would be a significant move in heightening his own status and worth. It was as though he were saying, "See what kind of sharp people my diocese produces!"

So, he set up a meeting between these fellows from his diocese and the cardinal who had let it be known that he was quite open to making their acquaintance. The meeting turned out the way they had hoped it would. The cardinal, coming face to face with Francis' disarming simplicity, took a liking to him. He entertained the group at his palace for a few days, offered them some advice, and tried to understand their dreams. At first he was somewhat fearful and anxious; but in the end, overcome by that genuine look in Francis' eyes, he spoke to the Pope about them. The audience was arranged.

Innocent III was a pope like few others. Politically speaking, many people consider his pontificate so important that history has not seen anything like it before or after. For sure, he was a man fully conscious of his own worth and perfectly aware of his own actions. Added to his strong character there was the noble way he carried himself and intense way he thought. He was a highly cultured gentleman and an author of ascetical and theological works. He also was inbued with that fine sensitivity of a poet and the very practical methods of a doer. He, moreover, had a touch of that pessimism which is characteristic of someone who knows people all too well and constantly is dealing with their underhanded tricks.

Before he became pope, his name was Lothar of the Counts of Segni. The cardinals elected him to the papacy on January 8, 1198, when he was only 38 years old. As it was, with the name of Innocent III, the youthful pope succeeded the elderly Celestine III.

Cardinal Lothar rose out of the divisions of the electors by virtue of his youthful age and also because of the quality of his innate energy and even-handedness. At this time, as successor of the old Pope Celestine, an energetic pope was sorely needed, one with clear ideas and quick decisions. This was a crucial time for the Church because rarely, if ever, had she had such an opportunity to be so involved on the world scene. It was something like the end of the tenth century when Gregory the Great and Gregory VII were in a similar situation.

From the point of view and the sensitivities of the 20th century, we could be scandalized or upset by what advantages the cardinal electors took or by what considerations motivated their behavior. But it would not be fair for us to do this. There is no need to ever judge (in the sense of condemn) history with the eye glasses of one's own age, and it is completely unjust to hand down some sort of moral judgment on the political and religious circumstances which were so very different from the reality in which we are called to live.

So, setting aside any judgment, let us attempt to look at how the meeting between the Pope and Francis came about. First of all, we have to keep in mind something which should be obvious but which we easily forget: if for Francis his kneeling before Innocent was a happening of great import, for the Pope, on the other hand, that audience (maybe there were more than one) was a very ordinary part of his style of administration. Taking into consideration these differences in importance and meaning for these two men, we have to try to know the person of the Pope himself so that we can understand better the various attitudes and reactions right at the very beginning which would color any future contacts between the liveliness of Francis and the structures and thought processes of the Roman Curia.

It seems that biographers, past or present have never paid much attention to the real happening of the episode. Rather, they have been content to interpret the meeting between Francis and the Pope either an as example of some sort of sugar-coated piety or as the beginning of an antagonism on the part of Rome toward the saint of Assisi. The concept of understanding vis-à-vis misunderstanding, or perhaps significant awareness versus ordinary happenings, right from the start was not taken into consideration. Yet, we know well that, even though language developed to help people understand each other better, it sometimes serves the purpose of hiding what we do not comprehend even though we are not conscious that this is happening. One of the most common expressions of scholastic philosophy goes something like this: "Whatever we perceive, we do so only insofar as we are prepared to understand it." Perhaps this will help to simplify the matter a bit and make the problem a little easier to understand. Now, however, it is appropriate to do some backtracking in history to shed a little better light on what we have to say.

The imperial crown whlch Pope Leo placed on Charlemagne's head on Christmas Night in the year 800 launched a grand political-religious process. I do not intend to talk about the power or the expansion of the Holy Roman Empire which only came about because of the strength of the individual emperors and their armies. Instead, I want to make reference to the great bank of ideas and concepts which each emperor was able to circulate throughout the Catholic world. Even today the "dream of Europe" which is still alive and well, has a direct connection with the dreams that were popular back then.

The tenth and eleventh centuries were certainly the most flourishing time for the Holy Roman Empire which was first based in France and later was headquartered in Germany. This empire, which ideally was to be one with the Church, had a dignified and sacred character and became tied up with every aspect of the medieval spirit. Envision a pyramid (this is a common image to describe the medieval world). At its top were the two leaders, the pope and the emperor – as it were, the incarnation of divine majesty. Below them in a hierarchical order (which sometimes conflicted for position) were dukes and archbishops, nobles and artists, and finally the ordinary people. This ideal world really worked and actually flourished as long as the emperors were clever enough not to oppose the ecclesiastical organization, or (to say it another way) as long as the pope was weak enough not to want to be more and more autonomous from the imperial authority. This latter scenario, for good or for ill, made both the clergy and the whole sphere of religion more secularized and worldly minded.

When, then, the emperors intruded too much into the

rightful affairs of a papacy, bent upon renewing itself by demanding that they be able to appoint local bishops and thereby take advantage of the accompanying benefits, there began a rivalry which brought about a dramatic split.

As the Church fought for its own freedom, it found that throughout Europe at that time there was a growing thirst for national and local liberty, which it both supported and promoted. So, the Church became the champion of a new social structure. Little by little it help cast off the fetters of medieval society and affirmed a freedom which up to that point had not yet been thought possible. In doing so, it held in check the controlling influence of the emperor.

This is why there was a popular consensus for what the Church was doing which resulted in its greater self-awareness as a power to bring people together. In order to continue to justify their own role of leadership, the clergy promoted theories and programs which spelled out the supremacy of spiritual power over temporal. It was not yet a popular point of view that the powers of the world were dependent upon those of the spirit, but soon Pope Boniface would claim this supremacy by placing himself above kings and emperor.

The most important document regarding such supremacy dates back to the beginning of 1303. This is the papal bull entitled *"Unam Sanctam"*. This quarrel, which actually seems to have little connection with spiritual values, developed within the Church a great sensitivity to the challenges of the Gospel. The freedom preached in the name of the Gospel led people to a re-reading of that same Gospel. New and different mystical movements appeared on the scene, and some of them strayed from the Church's foundation of orthodoxy. In this climate of unrest the official Church was, at the very same time, both an object of protest and a protest itself; it promoted new freedoms and reacted against too much freedom.

It supported the strengthening of the communes' freedom; but, as a central power in its own right, it did not accept any challenges against its own supremacy.

Moreover, even within the Church's hierarchy there was a constant clash between religious feelings and a thirst for power. Some bishops and ecclesiastical dignitaries were hostile to other bishops and people of importance. It is no wonder, then, that between the eleventh and thirteenth centuries there was the flowering of a great religious revival which ended up as real and wide-scaled heresies. A Church which was trying to distance itself from a sacral-imperial approach to running the Christian world found itself to be an easy target of that same religious spirit which it was stirring up.

The heretical movement was quite extensive and came from far distant places. As easy as it is to make this simplification, it is not meant to be deceptive. For example, the heretical strain of the Cathari was fundamentally different – because of its dualistic origins and its Manichean approach to interpreting life – from the movements of poverty which came out of another cultural origin and certainly was not born of the heretical or schismatic desire to confront the Roman Church.

This movement to be poor was rooted in a cultural foundation that had a Christian inspiration. In itself it was quite a legitimate rebellion against all the corruption within the visible Church. It was a protest against excessive riches and the longing for power. The more violent the protest became, the more easily did it become the beginning of a schism. A schism is not the same thing as heresy; but it can open the door to a heretical movement when, out of a sense of rebellion, a theological point of view turns into a doctrine which the Church considers unacceptable and wayward.

It would be interesting to follow these turn of events and to understand the reasons why they took place. Those reasons were often held with great passion and deep conviction, but they sometimes went too far, overstepping the limits of justice, when their provocation fractured the unity of the Church.

There are some poems from the part of France called Provence which present an elegy of rage and sorrow and which can be considered a true expression of the movement to embrace poverty. At the same time they show us how fragile a separation there is between protest, schism, and heresy:

"I am not surprised at all, O Rome,
if people fall into heresy,
because you have sent the world
into travail and wars.
Esteem and good will are dead and buried
on account of you, Rome, you deceiver,
for you are the guide, the summit, the root
of all evil.
The good king of England was betrayed by you. ...

Rome, I know for certain
that with your false assurance of pardon,
you have abandoned the nobility of France
to the fate of torment, far, far from Paradise. ...

Oh Rome, the Pope is wrong
when he disputes with the Emperor
for the rights of the crown,
proclaiming him a heretic and
pardoning those who fight against him.
Such an unreasonable forgiveness, O Rome,
is neither genuine nor legitimate".

(cf. "Poesie Provenzali Storiche," Vol. II, in *Fonte per la Storia d'Italia*, Ist. Stor. Ital., Roma 1931).

If we wanted to provide some evidence of the complaints against corrupted clergymen, we would have to add many more pages to this book. What was said above refers to Rome, but even more depressing and vulgar things were said about the monks, priests, abbots, and bishops.

So, one thing is very clear: this was a world in turmoil which wanted to renew itself. This world did not identify itself as some small, insignificant group of people, but rather a leaven to bring about the total reform of the Church. In this honest restlessness, if we sift out those who were complaining merely because of their own self-interest or profession we come face to face with those who felt the chasm very deeply, such as heretics and popes, mystics and bishops, monks and laity.

But if we look at this phenomenon from a different vantage point, in particular, from the perspective of the church hierarchy and especially from where the pope stood, we cannot help observing what was happening as a brooding menace to the stability of the Church. Because it was brooding, it was all the more frightening. Hence, it makes sense that there was a penchant for telling the difference between the good and the wicked, between people who were firmly on the side of fidelity to the Holy See and those who might be schismatics or heretics. The same reality, as seen from different points of view and, above all, from the varying perspectives of those in authority, presents to us separate faces.

Pope Innocent III was on the Chair of Peter, sitting in the middle of all this chaos. He was looking for a balance between faith and politics and for a stable grounding for the Church. Both would have to unify and strengthen the Church, which at that time was a very difficult ship to maneuver. Among the too many contrasting forces in opposition to each other, among the many religious movements, among the multiple "drifting mines" which the emperor placed in the path of the Church, among so many fulfilled and unfulfilled dreams and expectations, there was the pope with his own agenda to accomplish. And in doing so, he intended to give the emperor his due.

Many historians have spoken about the scandal of using Francis as a tool of the Roman Curia. Well, personally, I would not be shocked by the idea of a pope, situated in the middle of so entangled a mess, being able to think that he could serve his own position well by employing a person like Francis as one of many means of support for his ecclesiastical policy. Too often we confuse "use" with "serve"! Moreover, it was the responsibility of the people to keep the ship afloat; and, if he had an extra oarsman, all the better!

Now getting back to our consideration of those two famous people: Innocent the Pope and Francis the Penitent from Assisi. Regarding Innocent, we have delineated, even though summarily, the enormous problems he faced. Regarding Francis and his ideals, we already talked about this at length.

I stated above that popular expression from scholastic philosophy: "Whatever we perceive, we do so only insofar as we are prepared to understand it." Now we are going to use this concept while we observe the papal audience which Pope Innocent granted to Francis. Of course there is no verbatim of such an audience in the daily newspaper "Osservatore Romano" simply because the Holy See did not have such a daily record at that time. So, we will have to resort to some reports that did exist (all of which came from the vantage point of people who were not part of the Roman Curia) to see what information we can acquire through our own intuition.

When Cardinal John presented Francis to the pope, he said: "I have found an excellent man who desires to live according to the form of the Gospel and in everything to observe evangelical perfection. I am convinced that through this man our Lord will renew the faith of the Holy Church in the whole world" (3 *Comp.* 12:48).

The pope was struck by these words and was eager to meet Francis. When the penitent from Assisi stood before the pope, he did not demonstrate any sort of reverential fear, but rather explained with confidence and respect the experience of his own life and that of his companions. It was a boundless trust in the grace of God and in the possibility of human beings to allow him to observe the Gospel to the letter in order to make practical and feasible the whole Sermon on the Mount.

Francis spoke to the pope about poverty and humility, about a practical application of trust in Providence. It was a presentation so very different from someone whom we would ordinarily consider wise and sensible. A "wise man" (with worldly wisdom, St. Paul would say) just does not conceive of a life where rights and responsibilities are not written in a code of law but are simply the spontaneous result of the real lived-out experience of loving. Nor would he be in a position to comprehend how it could happen that power would lose its meaning and property would lose its security. Yet, this is exactly the kind of life which Francis and his companions were explaining to the pope and were asking him to approve because they had good reason to embrace it and Christ and his Church agreed with them.

Innocent III, however, was a wise man. His wisdom came not only from his cultural background or inner convictions, but also from the fact he knew people well. He had never met anyone like Francis before. No honest historian would doubt his own desire to reform the Church, nor would minimize his own spiritual life. As this sort of perceptive person, the wise pope listened attentively to all the crazy and fascinating things which Francis spoke about so openly. This is why he said what he did to them:

"Your plan of life seems too hard and rough. We are convinced of your fervor, but We have to consider those who will follow you in the future, and who may find that this path is too harsh" (3*Comp.* 12:49).

Innocent, who was a good pope, was thinking about the future in realistic terms. He had understood as much as his mentality enabled him to do in regard to Francis and his companions. That is, he found them to be enthusiastic fellows who were in love with the Gospel (and this pleased him very much because he was very sensitive to spiritual values). But it seemed that they were somewhat imprudent in wanting to found a community or a religious order only on the basis of their own enthusiasm and their confidence in God. Experience taught him that the Gospel and zeal were not enough to start a religious order. In order to support themselves and to carry out what they wanted to do, they also needed houses and land.

Placing himself within the context of a very long tradition with its own experience of living the Gospel, the wisdom of this good pope's thinking could only go so far. He could not even imagine that these penitents were not really coming to him to ask him to approve their new monastic order. They here coming to the Vicar of Christ simply to announce their plan for living. They were looking for the pope's okay so that what they were doing would be considered an "ecclesial act," as we would say today. Ecclesial acts imply the recognition of a particular charism on the part of the one who has the responsibility to make just that sort of acknowledgment.

If the pope could not fully understand the plan which Francis requested that was not yet completely spelled out in all details, so Francis found it equally difficult to understand why the pope could object to a demand as simple as wanting to follow the Gospel. This is why Francis, filled with hope and confidence in the head of the Church, insisted so stubbornly. His tenacity must have been very impassioned and effective because the pope dismissed him with the implied promise that the whole matter would eventually be clarified: "My son, go and pray to God that he may reveal whether what you ask proceeds indeed from his most holy will; and this in order that We may be assured that in granting your desire We shall be following the will of God" (3 *Comp.* 12:49).

Certainly the pope suspected that he was facing something brand new. For a mind as accustomed to legal clarity as his was, the proposal which the little man from Assisi set before him provided him with something of a mystery that he had to reflect on and think through. Besides, Cardinal John presented Francis to the pope (if the biographers are right) not as the would-be founder of a new monastery but as someone who wanted to bring to the world a new way of living the Gospel. If we are to take seriously what the first biographers said and the interpretation they put on the facts, I think that we could situate the famous dream about the Lateran collapsing within this atmosphere of papal uncertainty. It was a dream in tune with that plan to renew the Church which Innocent himself supported and promoted.

In fact, we read that the pope "had a vision that the church of Saint John Lateran was only saved from falling by being upheld on the shoulder of a small, insignificant man. He had awakened depressed and surprised, and, being wise and discreet, he had pondered long on the meaning of the vision. A few days later blessed Francis and the brothers came to him..." (3 *Comp.* 12:51).

Somebody might notice that I place Innocent's dream of what happened after the encounter with Francis and not before, even though this goes contrary to what is related in all the sources already cited. If the dream is really authentic, then it only takes on full meaning after the fact. Actually, it reveals quite a bit about how Innocent III felt and what he thought. He was preoccupied with the fate of the universal Church (as symbolized by St. John Lateran, the cathedral church of the city and of the world), and it was a logical and natural development that he would perceive in this little fellow Francis a support for his efforts at rebuilding the Church. Here was a new religious order – young and vivacious, persistent and idealistic enough to achieve its purpose. This would be the perfect pillar to hold up the Church which was falling into ruin. So, after repairing three little churches in Assisi, Francis now found himself to be part of the restoration of the whole Church. This time it was "Church" with a capital "C" and meant the fullest extent of that word. It seemed certain, then, in the pope's mind-set, Francis came to be seen as a point of support for the renewal of the Church.

Let us now take a look at the mind-set of Francis. After the pope counseled him to go and pray, the saint did exactly that; he collected his thoughts in the spirit of prayer:

God spoke to him in spirit by a parable: "A poor and beautiful maiden lived in a desert, and a king, seeing her beauty, took her as his bride since he was sure she would bear him splendid sons. The marriage contract was drawn up and the marriage consummated, and many sons were born. When they grew up, their mother said to them: 'My children, do not be fearful or diffident, for your father is a king. Go, therefore, to his court, and he will give you all you need.' When the king saw these children, he marveled at their beauty, and recognizing their likeness to himself, he said: 'Whose sons are you?' They answered that they were the children of a poor woman who lived in the desert; upon which the king embraced them joyfully, saying: 'Fear nothing, for you are my children: and seeing how many strangers eat at my table, you who are my lawful sons will do so with far greater right.' He embraced them joyfully and decreed that all his children by the woman of the desert be summoned to his court, and there be provided for."

In this symbolic vision which came to him while he was praying, Francis understood that the poor woman represented himself. When he finished his prayer, the saint went before the pope and described all the particular details of the parable which the Lord revealed to him. And then he added:

"I am that poor woman whom God in his mercy has loved and honored, and through whom he has begotten legitimate children. The King of kings himself has told me that he will provide for all the sons he wills to raise up through me; because if he cares for strangers, he will also do so for his own children. Since God, in his loving providence towards the whole human race, gives so many good things of the earth to the unworthy and to sinners, in far greater measure will he provide for evangelical men who deserve his favor" (3 *Comp.* 12:50-51).

So, Francis likewise had received special instructions from God. And, if, on the one hand, the dream expanded the pope's idea to include Francis' future in the service of the whole Church, then, on the other, the story that Francis told faced the questions that Pope Innocent had. His lack of certainty about what Francis wanted to do is explained quite explicitly in the account of the Anonymous Perugian: "Your life is too hard and severe if you wish to found a community possessing nothing in the world. Where will you obtain the necessities of life?" (7:34).

The meeting of the pope and the saint was like the two sides of a pair of scissors coming together. On the one side, it seems that the pope came to understand a bit more of what Francis was all about, on the other, Francis came to realize that he would be able to alleviate some of the worries or preoccupations of the pope. They both moved forward together because of their encounter and perhaps unknowingly cut out the pattern which would lay out along specific lines the original intuition of the son of Peter Bernardone.

The eventual rapport between Francis and the Roman Curia which began with that encounter is like a railroad line. In the future the engine, set in motion by Francis, would run faster and faster, making its way along the track. Every now and then, however, the rails will go off among the meadows and forests along valleys open to the sun and along steep ravines, sometimes, at least, to put back into the journey the thrill of the original dream. The popes would rather enjoy this lively, unpredictable, good-natured kind of gospel spirituality which through the centuries became known as "Franciscan spirituality."

"When the pope looked at Francis and saw him fervent in the love and service of God, in his own mind he compared his vision of the Lateran with that related by Francis and he began to say to himself: 'This is surely a holy and religious man by whom the church of God will be supported and upheld.' Then he embraced Francis and approved the rule he had written and gave him permission to preach penance to all; and this permission was extended to all the brothers who had the approval of Francis" (3 *Comp.* 12:51). The Holy Father then confirmed this approbation given to the new movement in a solemn consistory (or meeting) of cardinals.

So, as far as we know, this is the end of the story – later recounted after the death of Francis by the famous *Three Companions* – of that first memorable encounter between the pope and the Franciscan ideal already lived out by the twelve.

A MOMENT OF UNCERTAINTY

Pope Innocent approved Francis' Rule. It was an oral approval according to the spirit of the man from Assisi who was not interested in written documents. Just as he did not use any writing paper to ask the Pope for an opinion regarding his new way of living according to the form of the Gospel, so the saint did not sense a need to have anything more than the word of the Vicar of Christ. It was not the papal seal at the bottom of a piece of parchment which helped him to live as a Christian. Therefore, when he left the audience with the pope, he did so with a heart filled with joy.

That happy moment is discussed at length in his spiritual testament that he dictated before his death. And this is one of the few memories he has handed down to his followers to indicate how happy this period of life really was for him. In fact, if we read the Testament carefully, we notice how Francis mentioned just a few things about his life and that those few occurrences took place in a rather short span of time. He records his encounter with the leper; his discovery of the Eucharist as the living presence of Christ; the generosity with which those first companions left everything to follow the Gospel in the spirit of prayer, penance, and work; and finally the approval which the pope had given to his way of life.

"And after the Lord gave me brothers, no one showed me what I should do, but the Most High Himself revealed to me that I should live according to the form of the Holy Gospel. And I had this written down simply and in a few words and the Lord Pope confirmed it for me" (Test. 16-18).

What the pope approved was not one of the texts of the two rules which we have today; rather, it was a collection of quotes from the Gospel to indicate some of the starting points which he and his followers wanted as a plan for living.

Let us pause here a while to reflect upon the importance of what we are saying. It was not an accident that Francis placed the approval of the pope among his few recollections. In a document as important as the Testament, those things are noted which most accurately echo the real spirit of the person and which had the most crucial impact upon the person making the statement. Just taking this reality into consideration is not sufficient to focus the researchers attention on the reason and the relevance of the event, even from a psychological point of view. Now if some monumental work would have been accomplished, perhaps it would not have been necessary to write so many pages to discuss in detail the interaction between Francis and the church hierarchy.

In Francis' own religious experience the bishop of Assisi and Pope Innocent were highly esteemed and deeply appreciated in a way that could not be captured in a description by someone with merely a sociological point of view. A study of the ecclesiology regarding the place of the local bishop and the pope as the bishop of the universal church could be a big help in understanding Francis in this relationship with them, not so much as one of submission but rather as one of dialogue in the fullest sense of the term. So, we have to understand how the actual lived-out experience of religious life could be a better teacher of a Gospel-based ideology than many academic studies in a university setting.

The group of penitents said good-bye to Cardinal John and perhaps also to Bishop Guido. They took to the road, heading for Assisi, with the pilgrim staff in hand and no shoes on their feet. They were in no hurry. Medieval pilgrims were never in a rush. Sometimes their journeys lasted for days or months or even years. We who are accustomed to watching the clock and moving at high speeds cannot really understand what it means to travel on foot. Yet, we have to try to get into the experience if we want to enjoy, at least in part, their journey back home. It is only by getting into this mood that we can really have the experience of taking ourselves back into a time when the beginnings and ends of journeys and the times of departure and arrival were not governed by train stations and airports. We really do not pay attention to the world around us across which we travel all the time, and we would be lost without any road signs. It is still a mystery to me how, in the past, people could come and go, could find their way and arrive at their destination with no directions, no maps, and even sometimes no roads at all! It's not just a technical mystery; it is a psychological mystery as well.

Perhaps my reflection was helpful. Now I hope that we can stretch our imagination to enter into Francis' dimension of space and time and move along with his group of followers on the road that leaves Rome and heads north, passing through Assisi. Picture some carts, some donkeys, also some knights and merchants along the way. See, there is a village at the top of the hill, and there is a city that is large enough to be bathed in the midday sun. Look, the friars are traveling in a row, sometimes in twos, sometimes alone. They are not too far apart from each other because they like to pray together and share the joy and excitement of being together and heading in the same direction. Every now and then they would stop under a tree for the Liturgy of the Hours and perhaps, though rarely, they would eat a bit of bread which one of them had begged. When they met someone else along the way or came across people in the villages or at their cottages, they would take advantage of the opportunity to preach the Gospel.

One of the places they stopped to rest was documented by Thomas of Celano. They were in the vicinity of Orte. Probably they came upon a cave dug out of the hillside or found a dilapidated hut. They were not bound any schedule and their sole intent was to live the Gospel, so they were ready to consider this a suitable place for a lengthier stay. In fact, they stayed here fifteen days. They begged a little food to keep them going and enjoyed the honeymoon days of that life in fraternity newly blessed by the pope. When the two weeks were up, they set off again for Assisi. They visited the various towns and castles along the way and did not hesitate to stop to preach, as was their custom.

Living from day to day, they trusted in Divine Providence for their food and shelter. They took their cue from Christ himself who did not have a place of his own to lay down his head. They did not even think of owning a house or a permanent dwelling place since it was possible to communicate with God or to approach the brothers anywhere at all. Assisi, moreover, became no more than a place to pass through rather than a spot for settling down.

After Foligno and Spello, when they saw Mount Subasio once again with the familiar houses and towers of Assisi on its slopes, they stopped again at the first shelter they could find. It was Rivotorto, not far off the main road. The place was an abandoned hovel; it must have been absolutely miserable if they found it empty. It was a good place, for the twelve of them even though the quarters were so close that they could fit in only with difficulty. They moved in and, as best they could, marked off a narrow personal space for each one at the suggestion of Francis who "wrote the brothers' names on the beams of the hut so that each one, when he wished to sit or pray, should know his own place, and that no unnecessary noise due to the close quarters should disturb the brothers' quiet of mind" (3 Comp. 13:55).

It is a bit of a surprise that their time of silence and prayer at Rivotorto lasted as long as it did. They were used to apostolic journeys – to going out and returning back home. Now, instead, they had spent a good part of the summer there, and they were coming upon the winter in a life of prayer and meditation which could take on the impression of a more monastic style of living. Was this a time for Francis to take stock of the situation? Was it like those special moments in times past after he met the leper or after Christ spoke to him at the cross of San Damiano? Or was there developing in the group a sensitivity to a kind of life in community which was more characteristic of monks? Was Francis taking to heart the rather clear advice of Bishop Guido and Pope Innocent to find one's bearings in setting up this new religious community based upon extreme material poverty?

The reason they did not leave from or return to the Porziuncula could depend on the fact that they were creating a brand new situation for themselves. If they felt the need to find a place to stop for a while, this they could not do at the Porziuncula because it really was not theirs. Both the church and, above all, the building next to it were the property of the Benedictines. Rivotorto, on the contrary, was either an old unused leper colony (so it seemed) and hence belonged to no one or, perhaps more likely, was owned by one of the disciples or by one of their families.

Perhaps this is a question that we will never be able to resolve. What we can say is that, as a result of Rivotorto, the attitudes and the mentality of the group of twelve seemed to change quite a bit from those earlier days that they spent at the Porziuncula.

There is a certain event (we cannot pinpoint when it exactly happened) which, in my opinion, took place around this period of time in the lives of these twelve men. I say this because of the psychological impact it had upon the men. Let me, then, lay out a possible sequence of what was going on. This episode, though, might have happened in the fall of 1209 during a previous stay at Rivotorto.

Anyway, about the autumn of 1210, Emperor Otto IV was traveling not far from Rivotorto on the road heading south. He had passed by that same place earlier that year during September when he went to Rome to receive the imperial crown. This second time, however, he was not going to Rome but rather to Puglia with the hope of conquering that territory. He was invited there by a group of barons who wanted to liberate themselves from the youthful Frederick II, son of the dead emperor, Henry IV and of Constance, and legitimate heir of the Norman Kingdom. If he were to take over Puglia, Otto would bring together the Holy Roman Empire and the Kingdom of Sicily. The Pope did not want this; he tried to make sure it did not happen by giving the imperial crown to Otto IV and taking it away from Frederick II who by hereditary title was already the King of Sicily.

Otto IV turned the political plans of the pope upside down and shattered all of the reasons why the pope permitted him to ascend the throne. It was an about-face of enormous proportions! To carry out his plans, he moved quickly from Pisa (where he had been staying) to overtake Puglia. Along the way he decided to stake his claim on the Duchy of Spoleto which was already an object of friction between the pope and the emperor. So, the emperor, meanwhile, made the Count of Acerra, Diepold of Schwienspeunt, who headed that group from Puglia, the duke of Spoleto.

The pope decided to excommunicate him for what he had done – a very serious matter in those days.

The context of these events and, in particular, that of the emperor's excommunication increased the importance of what now happened on the road near Rivotorto.

The emperor with his army marched toward Puglia. When an emperor passed by, there was great commotion not only because he was some important person but also because he had with him this retinue of dignitaries and soldiers which certainly did not make the peasants and the villagers along the way any too happy. The blasts of the trumpets, the pomp and ceremony, the evident signs of power all bothered Francis immensely. I have already said that his conversion to poverty had also caused a psychological change in his attitude toward power and the manifestation of power. You can imagine what an immense contrast there must have been between the contemplative world of the twelve in their serenity at Rivotorto and the world of the emperor which was keen on showing off the signs and symbols of an earthly power that Francis and his companions had given up.

Because of all the hoopla and the emperor's famous excommunication and not because of any contempt for authority (that was not his way of thinking), the saint prohibited his companions from going out onto the street to enjoy the unusual spectacle. He did make an exception for one of the fellows (we do not know whom) who was sent out to meet this important person in order that he could "continually call out to the emperor that his glory would last but a short time" (1 Cel. 43). The predetermined friar set off obediently to carry out the mission entrusted to him. With a prophetic gesture, he positioned himself in the middle of the street as though to stop the procession, and he raised his hand as a sign of condemnation or warning. In those days it was not very difficult to pull off this kind of public spectacle and to catch the attention of the emperor. The security guards did not have the kind of preventive measures which we would use today. So, Otto IV could well have heard what the friar said, and perhaps he "knocked on wood" so that it would not happen. He probably did not take this event too seriously. That kind of a nuisance was very common in those days, and he had probably run into more than a few of them as he traveled around. An incident like this would not have been an out-of-the-ordinary occurrence for that period of time.

After telling the whole story, Thomas of Celano contended that for Francis "the apostolic authority was strong in him, and he therefore refused entirely to offer flattery to kings and princes." My opinion is quite different. In fact, it is just the opposite.

I do not see the situation as one power against another power. What I see is the conflict between lack of power and possession of power. The different interpretations of this one single fact may well be a sign of the wide variety of interpretations regarding Francis' life in general.

As we said before, the group spent quite a long time at Rivotorto. Summer turned into autumn with its characteristic red foliage and ploughed fields. The little community of Rivotorto took turns dividing its time between begging alms and doing some work which would bring in a bit of payment as the farmers could afford. They pooled their resources and shared them among the members of the community. Their principal occupation, however, was prayer and meditation. Francis tried to teach his companions by sharing with them what little or how much he himself experienced in his prayer and in his personal contact with God. He instructed them to meditate and to do what was necessary in examining their consciences in order to avoid that misuse of time and talent or the coldness of heart which can take hold of those who have decided to devote their lives to God. Whenever there was some sort of conflict among the men, it was Francis who demonstrated how one who serves the Lord should act toward his brothers.

But the most humbling and trying difficulty was to go asking for alms. Even though they were holy men and loved the Lord very much, they just were not used to begging. The jeering of their relatives and friends and the crude insults of the townsfolk put them down psychologically. It was not good will they were lacking; it was thick skin to withstand humiliation. Francis, who was always sensitive to the difficulties of his followers, spoke to them about poverty. And, since he was the one who determined who went out begging when, he also took up the topic of obedience:

"If a brother, subject to a brother superior, not only hears his voice, but even understands his will, he must immediately give himself entirely to obedience and do what he understands him to do by some sign or other" (1 *Cel.* 45).

So great was the devotion of these twelve men for their guide that they had a supernatural revelation:

"For while, kindled by the fire of the Holy Spirit, they chanted the Our Father, not only at the appointed hours, but at all hours, with suppliant and melodious voices, being little occupied with earthly solicitude and troublesome anxiety of cares, the most blessed father Francis absented himself one night from them in body. And behold, about midnight, when some of the brothers were resting and some were praying in silence with great devotion, a most splendid fiery chariot entered through the door of the house and turned around two or three times here and there inside the house; a huge globe of light rested above it, much like the sun, and it lit up the night. The watchers were dazed, and those who had been asleep were frightened; and they felt no less a lighting up of the heart than a lighting up of the body. Gathering together, they began to ask one another what it was; but by the strength and grace of that great light each one's conscience was revealed to the others. Finally they understood and knew that it was the soul of their holy father that was shining with such great brilliance and that, on account of the grace of his understanding purity and his great tenderness for his sons, he merited to receive such a blessing from God" (1 *Cel.* 47).

This vision is in complete harmony with the admiration which the disciples had for their master who more and more was taking on the image of a spiritual guide, of a shepherd, and, we might add, of a superior or "abbot" of a new community.

For Francis, life at Rivotorto was not a bed of roses. If this place was supposed to be a kind of a "monastery," it was so small that it proved to be too impractical to allow anybody interested in looking over their way of life to join them. Besides, there was no chapel or church in which they could gather to chant their morning prayer or to pray the Liturgy of the Hours. Added to this concern and to the problem of supplying a ready food supply for all those holy young men who had devoted themselves to prayer and quiet, there was another worry, perhaps less noticeable but even more serious: hostility.

Perhaps near that place (as was already indicated) there were the lands and property belonging to the families of some of the friars. Quite likely the actual hovel they were staying in was owned by one of their families who expected that they would have to turn over the hut and the surrounding land to the community at Rivotorto if, perchance, it were to consolidate and strengthen its position by turning itself into a monastery.

So, it seemed right to get rid of the new community at Rivotorto.

In a short span of time, various difficulties disturbed Francis so that he did not exactly know what would happen next. The old enthusiasm for preaching the Gospel, the warmth of meeting each other along the way, and their successful plans of action which followed their gatherings were now just a memory. They were replaced by an ascetical life of penance with some sporadic preaching in the city, but this was not exactly what he had in mind. It is true that the friars were as fervent as ever in terms of their prayer and their penances, but these things they could have done in some other monastery wherever. He did not have to go to Rome to dazzle the pope in order to retreat to a monastery no matter how poor it might be.

Francis remembered that time when "one night around midnight, when all were sleeping on their poor straw mattresses, one of the brothers began to cry out: 'I am dying! I am dying!' Blessed Francis got up and said: 'Get up, Brothers; bring a light!' A torch was lit and blessed Francis asked: 'Who cried out: I am dying?' One brother said, 'I did.' And blessed Francis said to him: 'What ails you, Brother? What are you dying from?' 'I am dying of hunger,' be answered. Blessed Francis, a man full of charity and discretion, did not want the brother to blush from eating alone. He had a meal prepared then and there and everyone partook of it" (*Leg. Perug. 1*).

After the meal the saint preached a sermon, warning them to be moderate in carrying out their penance and urging them to do what is necessary to take care of their bodies.

That episode left a bitter taste in his mouth. Up until that time nothing like this had ever happened before. Their life had been much less complicated. When they were hungry, it was because they had nothing to eat and not because they weakened themselves with harsh penances. Certainly that brother abstained from food to fulfill a spiritual purpose and to demonstrate his love for God. Francis, however, felt that this was not the right path to follow.

As we have seen, there were many problems, and they had to be resolved pretty quickly. We cannot say for sure what happened and how things turned out. The biographers relate, however, that Francis proposed to his companions that they go to the bishop or to the canons of the cathedral or to the abbot of Mount Subasio to ask for "a small and poor church where the brothers may recite their Hours and, next to it, a small and poor house built of earth and wood where the brothers can sleep and go about their work" (*Leg. Perug.* 8).

After receiving a negative response from the bishop and from the canons, he got a positive answer from the Benedictine abbot of Mount Subasio who gave Francis the little church of the Porziuncula, provided that he would make it the center of all his future activity.

On the surface, the group was finally moving because of a lack of space after being at Rivotorto for a number of months. We do not exactly know how it all came about. Such was the state of affairs when at this point in history there came upon the scene a providential donkey which cut short their doubts and uncertainties.

SOME NEW POSSIBILITIES FOR THE
WORLD

I n wintertime the confined quarters of Rivotorto had its advantages. For one thing, it did not let in more cold air than the heat of their bodies could ward off. So, at least they found some comfort amid all the excessive hardship they had to suffer.

One day they were gathered together in prayer when they heard this most unpleasant and vulgar noise. A few moments later, the door burst open and there stood that noise right in the middle of the doorway. A farmer entered with his donkey, screaming and shouting at the animal, "Get in there. We will put this hole to good use." While yelling, he slapped the reluctant beast on the backside, and immediately threw the whole place into utter confusion.

Those young men acted like saints. In fact, they did not raise a hand against the farmer nor did they kick the donkey. They put up with the whole thing patiently and quietly. Francis all of a sudden saw how to resolve the situation at hand—he had absolutely no doubt that the intrusion of the donkey and its master was an expression of God's will for him. He said they were right in ordering them to pack up and go. They had so little to take with them that they were soon ready to go. The community left the place to the donkey.

With a renewed spirit of adventure, they headed a bit

north toward the little church of St. Mary of the Porziuncula where they had stayed before. As was mentioned in the previous chapter, this place was given to them by the Benedictine abbot of Mount Subasio. Near the church was a covered building that would be somewhat comfortable in winter. It was convenient to have a church so close at hand. With simplicity they settled into the place, just as they had occupied the hovel at Rivotorto.

The mind-set of Francis excluded in any way, even the thought of private property. So, when he came upon a different place, he laid no claims upon it; he just used it as he found it. Nonetheless, at the Porziuncula he could not get away from addressing the question of ownership. He knew well that the church and the adjoining building were the property of the Benedictines. St. Francis had high regard for the Benedictines who more than once welcomed him with open arms and helped him most willingly. And for this reason he wanted to pay rent for the place with a basketful of fish from the Tescio River. In a gesture of esteem and love the monks, in turn, gave Francis a container full of olive oil.

We have already had the chance to note that the reasons why the group moved from Rivotorto to the Porziuncula were not clear-cut. Likewise, we are not exactly sure why the monks of Mount Subasio were willing to turn this property over to the friars, especially after they got the same negative response to their request from the bishop and from the canons of St. Rufino.

Those readers familiar with the early Franciscan writing realize that Thomas of Celano situates this move to the Porziuncula just after the intrusion of the donkey and the farmer.

The *Legend of the Three Companions*, however, has the request to the abbot placed after the arrival of the donkey and before the group was kicked out. The *Legend of Perugia*, on the other hand, seems to ignore the story of the donkey and the farmer all together. Whatever the actual cause of the move may have been, it appears that it was very much on purpose to highlight the Porziuncula as the central focus of the Franciscan Order and as the source of inspiration for all those who had followed the experience of the saint of Assisi.

So, it seems quite natural that the story of asking the bishop and the canons and the abbot for a church would receive such a build-up. This probable development of events was more of a symbolic nature than historical fact in order to underline clearly the idea that the plan of God was being realized in the friars' choice of a place where they got their start; namely, the Porziuncula. This, in fact, for Francis and his first followers, is where they started their love affair with the Gospel and where they discovered their new way of life. For the second generation of friars, however, the Porziuncula had a different meaning: it was the model of the Order of Friars Minor, a place of devotion, an example of prayer and poverty. And down through the centuries the little church would become a multi-faceted symbol to express and make present the values which had been enfleshed in the experience of St. Francis. It would be the place where the Gospel was rediscovered, where the saint of Assisi lived and died, where the devotion to Mary took shape, where reconciliation happened (that is, the famous indulgence granted by Christ and the Church at the request of Francis in his concern for the salvation of all people).

If the time at Rivotorto was a period of deep reflection and perhaps the experience of the contemplative dimension of his life-style, the return to the Porziuncula was for Francis a return to his most basic inspiration to live according to the Gospel. The *Legend of the Three Companions*, in fact, attributes these words to Francis to explain the move to the Porziuncula:

"Dear Brothers, I know that God has not called me to entertain a donkey and to get all tangled up with the affairs of people, but to show others the way of salvation by preaching and wise counsel. We must, therefore, above all, make sure of being able to pray and give thanks for the graces we receive.' So they left the hut which later was used by poor lepers, and they moved to St. Mary of the Angels, the Porziuncula; nearby was a little dwelling in which they lived before they received the church itself" (3 *Compa. 55-56*).

We have the impression that Francis left behind in the very walls of Rivotorto the urge to turn the movement he created into a monastic style of living. The fact of the matter is that, as soon as Francis and his companions returned to the Porziuncula, they seemed to return to that original way of living with which they started. They went back to their overriding calling of preaching that new life found in the Gospel while in their day-to-day living they became more concerned with the bigger picture and less taken up with trivial details.

People, in addition, who were enthralled by Francis began to show up at the door of the church. They came down from Assisi, they arrived from nearby villages, they traveled from cities far away. They were fascinated by this new way of living. Many of them placed themselves at the disposal of this young leader. The newcomers stayed with the work they were doing if it was a humble sort of job. In the instances where they had some important kind of position, they learned to do something new. When it was necessary they would travel around Umbria or went even further to communicate their own experiences, to work for a living, and, if the work they were doing was not bringing in a sufficient wage, to go begging. For example, when Giles was in Puglia, he got a job transporting water in containers throughout that dry countryside so that he would not be an economic burden on the people to whom he was explaining this new way of life.

Every now and then they felt the call to return to the Porziuncula, and they longed to come back together and share their experiences while they gathered on the plain below Assisi. And after a short time they set off again, only to return once more. Here they were unfettered wanderers who were completely taken up with the new work which Christ and Francis had found for them.

The number of disciples increased, and hence the radius of their activity grew larger. They touched upon new cities and castles and, by the same token, came upon new problems and situations. At that time the matter of concern for many people was this: in order to live the Gospel, did the people have to leave their spouses and children and fields and jobs? Up till then, anyone who set out to change one's life had left everything, and none of them were married. Under these conditions it was not difficult to wander about, ready to respond to every inspiration. But if this life which they had discovered was suitable for everyone and no one was to be excluded since all were called to follow this way, how could it be a possibility for those who had a wife or a husband or little children, for those who were involved in the different fields of labor, for those who were conducting honest business?

Someone brought this to Francis' attention, and he – as he was in the habit of doing – resolved the matter in a way that was simple and realistic as he had learned to do from Sacred Scripture and from his own personal experience. The life he proposed to them was brand new and required a total dedication. Actually it was nothing more than following the teachings of Christ himself. Not all of the disciples of Jesus were sent throughout the world. Mary herself, the Mother of Christ, remained at home and took care of the domestic chores. Only a few times do we find her with her Son. To be a Christian did not mean to travel about the world but to make practical all of the values which are presented in the Beatitudes. If a person is not in love with earthly power nor is overcome by the influence of money nor holds to the belief that he or she is superior to another; if someone is willing to share with one's neighbor and is content with working every day to get enough food to eat; if he or she is not looking for justice only from the human point of view but is a person of peace; if such a one is in love with having things clear and bright and is enthusiastic for God – then that person is already living the new way of life! Try to live that way, and you will be doing what Francis has been preaching.

The recipe was basically simple. It was the same thing which had been written about for centuries by those concerned with the Gospel. But too few people took the risk of seriously giving it a try either because of laziness or fear; and they just were not aware of what they were missing! Holiness is not the prerogative of just monks and bishops; it is the daily way of living for everybody!

What Francis was saying was simple and obvious. But it surely caused a sensation in those days, just as it still does today, because it was as revolutionary as the miracle or mystery of producing life. This was a revolution because it took Christianity as an intellectual conviction and made it plausible by turning it into a practical, everyday way of living.

Some people, who ordinarily do not completely understand the way Francis operated, would consider the events at this period of time as the definitive organization of that which would be called the Third Order of St. Francis and eventually would change its name to the Secular Franciscan Order. Though this might give evidence of the early indications of the "Brothers and Sisters of Penance" (the first name for the Secular Franciscan Order or Third Order), its formal organization came later.

It is not easy to list how many apostolic journeys Francis made. We can say, however, that his biographers developed the penchant for setting all of his wanderings within the framework of miracle and marvelous events. The humble and ordinary mission of the man was beginning to be presented as the triumphant journey of a saint. So, to keep our feet on solid ground, it could be said that during his journeys Francis preached, prayed, went to the public squares, and slipped away to deserted places, as the necessity arose. But it is obvious that, with the passage of time, the saint's fame grew among the people, and they came to pay their respects to him. So too did the problems increase!

Once he returned to the Porziuncula there followed a fifteen year period of his life in which were interwoven joys and sorrows, successes and failures, enthusiasm and discouragement. In other words, after the bubbling joyfulness of those days in the beginning, he settled into the life of an ordinary human being.

It was about this time, around the year 1212, that Francis felt the urge to preach the Word of God not only in Italy among the Christians but in Syria among the Moslems. This is the first time that the man of God was interested in being a missionary. Perhaps this is connected with the enthusiastic response to the crusade which was developing at that time. But Francis' desire did not really have anything in common with the spirit of the crusades as such. It was even quite likely that he wanted to do something in reaction to the methods of the crusades.

So, it was his desire to get a taste of someplace outside of his own territory, some foreign country with a different religion and culture. So, from Assisi he started off toward a port on the Adriatic where he could embark upon a ship heading east.

The traffic between Italy and the Middle East was more developed than we might think, and many merchant ships and many other vessels left for the East, enjoying the relative calm of coastline sailing. A few years ago Luciano Canonici advanced an hypothesis which is worth sharing: he thought that Francis left from the coastal town named Ortona in the territory of Abruzzo where he found some good connections for travel. Perhaps he was granted free passage for the love of

God or perhaps be worked as a cabin-boy. Whatever the case, he was braving the seas for the very first time in his life.

It was not a pleasant experience at all! The ship immediately found itself right in the middle of a storm. It was tossed about and dragged through the Adriatic while the people prayed and cursed in absolute terror. Finally, when the ship broke free of the clutches of the storm, it landed on the coast of Slavonia, today called Dalmatia. It did not seem that Francis took advantage of this unanticipated port of call to do any extensive preaching in this country which was unknown to him. Instead, he set out to find a ship that would take him to Ancona. He did not have the money to pay for the journey; so it was clear to him, one more time, that he naturally would have to call on the mercy of God or would have to work in exchange for passage. At least he did not get on ship as a stowaway (and he was capable of doing that!). By the grace of God, he reached Italy.

The journey, which at first was more of a negative experience than a misfortune, turned out to be a blessing from God because he was needed back home. He went back to Assisi, and there he faced the problem which was developing in regard to Clare of Favarone who belonged to the family of counts of Sassorosso.

There is a Latin saying ("quod differtur non aufertur") which, loosely translated, means, "You can put off solving problems, but you can never really get rid of them."

Up until 1212 the movement started by Francis was made up of predominantly (but not exclusively) male members. The women in those days were always in the background, not in the sense that they held no responsibilities of importance (cooking is very important!), but rather, simply put, they were not taken into consideration. This was because, given the social situation of that era, women just could not have done the same things which Francis and his companions were allowed to do. At most, women would number among those who supported him and agreed with what he was doing; and perhaps it was just for their sake that Francis made it very clear how it was not necessary to leave home, in order to live the Gospel according to his new way of life.

But when this beautiful, noble, enterprising, enthusiastic, headstrong, blond (if the hair preserved is really hers) young woman – Clare of Favarone, daughter of the nobleman Offreduzzo – was convinced that she was going to live the Gospel in exactly the same way as Francis, all the plans he had in mind had to be abandoned. This young woman wanted to change her life, and wanted to do so by leaving home for something brand new. Secretly she had spoken to Francis about this. They had to speak in secret (with the help of Christiana, the daughter of a nobleman named Bernard of Suppo, who was Clare's lady-in-waiting and later became a nun at San Damiano), because they did not want to stir up any gossip that would irritate the family.

Francis urged Clare to stay at home and live a life of virtue and chastity. He did not know what else he could propose. Taking her away with him would have been sheer folly. In the end, the bishop got into the middle of this whole situation. Bishops, when they so desire, are able to untangle any situation. And Bishop Guido, who had been present at that crucial moment when Francis severed the ties with his own family, now was there for Clare to give her the counsel and support she needed.

The three of them – the bishop, Francis and Clare – put their minds together to orchestrate a plan of escape. It would be better if such a plan were organized and directed by an important person like Guido, rather than just taking off in some spirited, though ill-advised, way.

The day was Palm Sunday. The bells of the cathedral of San Rufino rang out to call the people to Mass celebrated by the bishop. Everyone knew that palms would be distributed and that this would be the beginning of the festivities for

Holy Week. The people arrived, ready to celebrate this feast-day. They were dressed in their finest clothes, rich in color. Ladies and gentlemen and young girls took their places in the cathedral according to their rank of importance. There was the rustle of conversation up until the time the episcopal ceremonies began. The palms were carried into the church, and the bishop blessed them invoking God's name and recalling the shouts of "Hosanna!" given to Christ. Then the people came to the communion rail to receive the palm they would carry in procession and take to their homes as a symbol of the Easter mysteries. Everyone was moving about. Except Clare. She stood still at her place, deep in ecstacy.

The bishop was well aware of her excitement and her anxiety. He waited in vain to give her the palm. He was planning to give her a rather large palm branch. The people would be thinking that this gesture was a sign of distinction to recognize the daughter of the Offreduccio Family, while it really had quite a different meaning. When the last of the young women and men approached the bishop and Clare still had not moved, Bishop Guido came down from the altar vested in his episcopal finery and walked over to Clare to offer her the sign of peace and the blessed branch of palm. Clare was slightly startled. She took the palm from the bishop, conscious of the meaning of this gesture. Then the ceremonies continued with the various liturgical chants and prayers.

At nightfall Clare went down the hill to St. Mary's of the Angels. Common sense cannot explain her running away from home, out of the so-called "door of death," to the little church in the valley. She abandoned her known rich surroundings for something unknown. She gave up a fine reputation for the risk of an adventure that did not even have a clear direction.

She sprung open the "door of death," which was that exit from the palace used exclusively for the removal of dead bodies, so that she would not carry with her all the unwelcome baggage of life in the world. She intentionally passed through that door to signify her irreversible choice; she was not going to look back. It was difficult for her to open that door, but in the end she managed. Sister Christina, who was the thirteenth witness in the process of canonization, recalled that on the door "there were some heavy pieces of wood and a stone column. It took a well-built man to remove these things. But she did it by herself, with the help of Jesus Christ, and she flung open the door."

She arrived at the Porziuncula. Francis and his companions were there waiting for her. They were all somewhat uneasy because of the unaccustomed presence of this gentle woman. They escorted her into St. Mary of the Angels, lighting her way with a lamp. Clare knelt before the altar. Francis, in the name of God, cut her hair as a sign of consecration. She could not be denied the grace of serving her Lord God. Human reasoning no longer had any value in this instance, just in the same way that Francis saw no advantage in accepting the common sense of Pope Innocent. But the validity of her choice did not stop the embarrassing effect which her decision had. Francis' radical confidence in the Providence of God did not prevent him from suffering hunger pangs. In the same way, the choice of Clare and her determination did not take away from Francis the apprehension of having a noble and beautiful young woman right there among all of the holy men of the Porziuncula. He could think of a better solution than this:

After "tonsuring" Clare at the altar of the Porziuncula (that is, after she was consecrated to God by the symbolic snipping off of her hair), she would be immediately escorted to the monastery of Benedictine nuns called St. Paul's in the vicinity of Bastia. As we can see, many people are involved in Clare's departure from the world.

Thus, Francis and Clare meet one another again as companions and victims of the same destiny: society was not willing to try something new, so it was virtually impossible to implement in an outward life-style that which their creative ingenuity called for but which society's common sense would strongly object to. Francis was "tonsured" by Pope Innocent and thus he was made a "cleric"; Clare was "tonsured" by Francis, and thus she became a nun.

Today, even though we have open to us many other avenues to understand and get involved in the social situation, still perhaps we might not have acted any differently. So, we have to admit that the restrictions placed on us by society have had and will continue to have a certain influence in our lives.

From the Monastery of St. Paul, Clare moved to the Monastery of San Angelo di Panzo near Assisi until her sister Agnes and some other women came to join her. Then Francis transferred her to the little church of San Damiano – that very place where he as the young son of Peter Bernardone had heard the voice of Christ crucified and which he had rebuilt by collecting stone and mortar.

At San Damiano's Clare and the sisters, guided by Francis, would have had to develop their own lifestyle. And precisely because they were able to set up their own way of living according to the Gospel in a poor and innovative manner, they had no one to put their confidence in except God alone. This is why Francis called them "Ladies."

Clare and her companions settled into San Damiano and turned that place into a center of spirituality, which caught on so quickly that in just a few years throughout Italy and the other countries of Europe the number of houses were growing to accommodate all those women who began to fall in love with this new way of life.

There is a small sign which testifies to this vitality: the four original letters which Clare wrote to Agnes of Prague, the daughter of King Ottocaro I of Bohemia, who had refused to marry two rulers in order to follow the daughter of the noble-man Favarone. There is also another letter (which, though generally considered authentic, does raise some questions in parts of the text) addressed to Ermentrude of Bruges who took on the responsibility of bringing the way of life from San Damiano's even to faraway Flanders.

Francis knew that the revelation of God contained in the Bible had to be interpreted in the light of human nature and the reality of the world. He was quite clever in doing that. He was able to grasp the teachings of God so well that he could express them in concrete life situations and explain them in a way that people understood. He was probably not even aware that he had attained such a comprehensive approach to actu-ally living life to the fullest, that there were not any inconsis-tencies in that overall harmony between all the elements of his existence.

Not everything, however, was fine and dandy! Francis was still perplexed regarding some of the decisions he had to make about his own life. During this period of time various thoughts and feelings were beginning to emerge inside of him. So many people wanted to get his attention and to tell him what he had to do and where he ought to go that at times he just could not figure out what to do. Doubts provoked by other people surfaced in his mind, but he did not try to sweep them under the rug because he believed that he had to dis-cover the will of God not only through prayer and meditation but also through the multitude of experiences happening in everyday human life.

What was he to do? Had he been on the right course up till now? Was the 180-degree turn he made after abandoning the place at Rivotorto a change for the better? What really did he prefer – a life of solitude? a life in community? a life of evangelizing while wandering around the world?

The uncertainty must have been driving him crazy if, as we

read in the Fioretti, he felt the need one day to discover the will of God. This was a crucial moment of his life, comparable to that time when he found the answer to his questions by paging through the Gospels at random after calling on the Holy Spirit to help him.

Hence, Francis "was placed in a great agony of doubt as to what he should do- whether to give himself to continual prayer or to preach sometimes. He wanted very much to know which of these would please Our Lord Jesus Christ most. And as the holy humility that was in him did not allow him to trust in himself or in his own prayers, he humbly turned to others in order to know God's will in this matter.

"So he called Brother Masseo and said to him: 'Dear Brother, go to Sister Clare and tell her on my behalf to pray devoutly to God, with some of her purer and more spiritual companions, that He may deign to show me what is best: either that I preach sometimes or that I devote myself only to prayer. And then go also to Brother Sylvester, who is staying on Mount Subasio, and tell him the same thing."

So Brother Masseo went to ask Clare who was at San Damiano's and to ask Sylvester who was in solitude and prayer in one of the caves on Mount Subasio where the surface of the mountain split open just a bit to form somewhat of a gorge. When Francis saw Masseo returning, he got down on his knees and pulled his hood up over his head as a sign of deep reverence for the response of God and for the one who carried that message.

"St. Francis asked him: 'What does my Lord Jesus Christ order me to do?' Brother Masseo replied that Christ had answered both Brother Sylvester and Sister Clare and her companion and revealed that 'He wants you to go about the world preaching, because God did not call you for yourself but also for the salvation of others.' And then the hand of the Lord came over Francis. As soon as he heard this answer and thereby knew the will of Christ, he got to his feet, all aflame with divine power, and said to Brother Masseo with great fervor: 'So let's go – in the name of the Lord" (*Fior.* 16).

And right then and there, he set out to preach with Masseo at his side. It is interesting to note that "right now" approach which is so characteristic of Francis. It is both a psychological and material readiness so typical of those people who do not have anything to pack nor any business to take care of before they leave.

Francis was on his way.

Miracles about the saint started to abound. People were saying that he spoke to animals and to the birds who filled the air with all their chirping and chatter. "My sisters the birds," he would say, "you ought to give praise to the God who created you. He is the one who has fed you and clothed you." And the birds would nod their heads and jump for joy until the saint let them fly away freely across the sky. Or there was the story about Francis making peace with the famous wolf at Gubbio in behalf of the terror-stricken people of the town. The wolf gave Francis his paw as a sign of friendship, and the citizens promised to feed it. And then they treated it with respect and veneration as though it were a living relic of the holiness of Francis himself.

Literature is full of delightful and poetic stories about Francis which always seem to have a touch of sweet sentimentality. They testify to the admiration which the people had for the person of Francis, and they say something about how really special this man was. Legends are always based on the historical facts contained within them, just as fairy tales are not born out of nothing but develop from that inner richness manifested in dreams which cannot be brought to the surface by means of rational concepts.

About the year 1214 the man of God went to Tuscany to preach in the town squares where the citizens always seemed to be fighting with each other. But he never abandoned his old idea of taking the Gospel into the Islamic world. This was a personal commitment which he kept close to his heart but would not confess publicly. Since he was stopped from going among the Moslems by way of Ortona, he was now beginning to think about another way of getting there. Why not brave the journey by setting sail from a port in Tuscany, heading toward Spain, and from there going on foot to the faraway land of Morocco?

We may presume that his choice to head for Abruzzo was a way to bypass Assisi in order to find a port on the Adriatic coast to sail from. Likewise, his preaching tour in Tuscany could well have had a secondary motive: to set off for Spain. Of course this is only an hypothesis, pure speculation; but it is not proposed without any foundation.

Francis arrived in Spain. When he left from the Adriatic heading for the East, the adverse winds pushed the ship to Slavonia, thus preventing Francis from reaching his destination. Once more he had to give up his dream to go among the Moslems, and returned to Italy through France. Thomas of Celano was himself moved when, in relating this second failure of Francis, he briefly mentioned an instance from his own life: "But the good God, whom it pleased in his kindness to be mindful of me and of many others, withstood him to his face when he had traveled as far as Spain; and, that he might not go any farther, he recalled him from the journey he had begun by a prolonged illness" (1 *Cel* 56).

When he got back to the Porziuncula, Francis "welcomed with honor and dignity" a few learned men and some nobles who had requested to follow him. Among them was Thomas, who came from Celano, a fortress in the territory of Abruzzo.

BETWEEN GOD AND POLITICS

I n November of 1215 Francis was in Rome. After his first meeting with Pope Innocent in 1210, he returned to Rome in 1212, perhaps to update the pontifical curia, if he did not actually get to see the pope in person, regarding the developments that he and his companions had been experiencing.

On that occasion he made friends with a Roman noblewoman whom he would call, up till his death, "Brother Jacopa." Her husband, Gratian Frangipani, was a well-to-do patrician of a noble Roman family. At that time she was probably about twenty-five years old.

Francis was not used to considering the social standing of his friends and followers. Nor were the riches of this noblewoman a concern of his. The only thing that mattered to him was whether or not somebody really wanted to live the Gospel; nothing else was important. That willingness of his to accept anyone without any hard feelings toward the rich nor any favoritism toward the poor – characterized a man who had arrived at a certain balance in his life that was not overrun by emotionalism. He never showered certain privileges on a person because he or she was rich or even because he or she was poor. It was a person's first name that counted, not one's family name nor married name. In this way he interacted with people without snubbing the nobles and the moneyed class and without humiliating anyone else. He knew how to appreciate nobility and wealth when it was used for the service of God, but at the same time he did not underestimate the efforts of the poor to be at the disposal of their Lord.

Brother Jacopa was a woman of unquestionably high spiritual quality. She very noticeably detached herself from worldly concerns. Even though she had to administer her affairs according to the mentality of her day, nevertheless she did not let those things run her life. It seems that there was a fine tradition of generosity to the poor within the Frangipani Family, and this was quite significant in the thirteenth century society. For Francis the heart of this noblewoman was fertile ground to cultivate for the Lord.

When Francis came to Rome in 1215, the Fourth Lateran Council was beginning to take place in the city. It was convoked by Pope Innocent on April 19, 1213, and two years later its sessions were convened in the basilica of St. John Lateran. In fact, the exact date was the 11th of November, 1215. This was not a council that came about on the spur of the moment without any planning. On the contrary, it took two good years between the time it was announced and the time it was opened in order to make the necessary arrangements for the greatest number of participants possible to be present. This in itself shows how important Pope Innocent III considered this gathering to be.

The pope had called this council particularly for two reasons: the liberation of the Holy Land by means of the Crusades and the reform of the Church. These two problems were constantly occupying his mind during these years of his pontificate. He, in fact, really wanted to make those changes he considered necessary for the good of Christianity, and he wanted this to happen as quickly as possible.

What a massive assembly for the council, particularly considering the times! There were about 412 bishops coming from all over the Christian world, plus other invited guests and interested participants, both from the church's ranks and from civil society. There were about 800 abbots, religious superiors, and various delegates of rulers from the different republics and cities.

A council of this type today, from what little we know about it, would surely overwhelm us because we would be so taken up with the enormous amount of problems and concerns which the participants brought along with them. And what caused the problems and peaked the interest of people were not always of a spiritual nature. At least that is the way we would look at it now from our current point of view.

But that was then. Every age lives in its own culture, and it seems ridiculous to pass judgment on the cultural surroundings of another time, as though we could determine what was right and what was wrong.

Including the opening and the closing ceremonies, this council was made up of just three public sessions. These three official meetings were held, respectively, on November 11, 20, and 30 of 1215. The archbasilica of St. John Lateran was crowded with the delegates, the bishops, and curious onlookers. Besides all the ceremonies, the meetings were dedicated to some speeches and the approval of some resolutions from the work commissions. The council set the date to start the crusade: June 1, 1217. On that date the armies would gather in Sicily and would set sail from there. The pope would personally be on hand to impart his blessing. And, if necessary he would not simply bless them: "I am completely at your disposal," he stated during his opening discourse, "and, if I can be of any particular benefit to you, I am ready to personally support everything you do."

Besides the crusade, the council promulgated some decrees regarding the Church's relationship with the Greek Orthodox Church and regarding a clearer explanation of the Catholic faith. In terms of what pertained to the crusades, they had not

113

forgotten to take up the specific points of the venture's material interests; for example, protecting the possessions of the crusaders or considering how to put a stop to any possible maneuvers by profiteers. As for dealing with the Greeks, however, the council fathers, in anticipation of a reconquering of the Christian East in the near future (something near and dear to the pope), prepared the measures necessary to clarify various religious positions and political questions in view of reuniting the Eastern Church with the Western Church.

With a good deal of practical vision they tackled the boiling question of heresy in general and of the Albigensian heretics in particular. Also, the spirit of the crusades dominated much of their attention, probably more because of local concerns reflected at the council by individual bishops than because of a particular penchant of the pope. Among the various conciliar decrees we find one which might interest us specifically:

"In order to avoid serious confusion in the Church because of the wide proliferation of different religious orders, we prohibit the founding of new orders. Whoever would want to be a monk has to enter an order already established. Likewise, anyone who wants to begin a new religious community must accept the rule and the structure of one of the orders already approved" (Decree § 13).

This decree clashes a little with the concrete historical situation which itself was in the state of development. Or was this measure approved on purpose to avert a certain turn of events? There is no way of really knowing for sure.

Even before the Fourth Lateran Council was convened or got under way, the objective reality and the perceptiveness of the pope demanded some rather extraordinary interventions in order to give the Church a renewed vitality and greater sense of inner solidarity. The heresies and the indifference of church members were both becoming intolerable burdens. The shortage of anything to promote culture and the escalation of local concerns and problems frequently embittered both the individual diocesan churches and the Church worldwide and caused quite a bit of resentment.

In the face of this dire situation, the monastic orders – which were tied to the pope by the bond of obedience and were less closely associated with the individual diocesan bishops and completely free of their economic restrictions – were able to start the ball rolling to diffuse the various local difficulties and supply whatever was lacking to bring about the visible unity of the Catholic Church. And culture, naturally, depended a great deal on the monasteries which could be found in every diocese. It is quite obvious, then, that the pope counted quite a bit on the monks in the face of unbridled heresy and the poor quality of catechetics in too many of the local churches. It is equally obvious that the diocesan bishops were not too pleased with all this. They were the ones who tried to put a stop to the growth of religious orders which had ultimately made the relationship between the two types of clergy within a diocese very difficult indeed.

But if the bishops who had passed that decree were satisfied by it, other decrees were delicately making it quite clear that the pope's intentions were to involve the religious order in the work of church renewal. We have, for example, Decree § 10 which states that the bishop has the right to preach in his own diocese but must get help from someone else when by himself he is not able to do the job adequately. And also there are other decrees which call for teachers and schools of religion to be organized in every cathedral and major church of the diocese. How could the individual bishops dó all of this without asking for help from the monasteries?

Historians believe that during the time of the council both Francis and Dominic Guzman, founder of the Order of Preachers or the Dominicans, were present.

The reason why we could imagine Dominic being in Rome is very obvious: he, working together with Bishop Folco of

Tolone, had just committed a group of competent preachers to assist the local Church to weather the presence of the many heretics and protestors that existed in the area. Practically speaking, they were a model of what was being proposed to the council.

But what was Francis doing at the council?

He certainly was not the type of fellow who would go to Rome to enjoy gatherings of powerful and important people. Nor do I believe he would go there to look for peace and quiet. My question is this: what was Francis looking for in going to Rome? It is appropriate to ask this since he would prohibit his friars from asking for any type of favor whatsoever from the Roman Church and since, I feel, at that time he would not have even had the favorable contacts to make such a request. Would he not have been invited, perhaps informally or indirectly, by the pope himself? The idea could seem rather absurd. But perhaps it is not that bizarre after all.

We have already spoken about the meeting between the pope and Francis. We have also taken into consideration how the pope would have pictured Francis' movement from his point of view. Now five years later, the experience of the penitent of Assisi was more mature, its credibility had grown immensely. For Pope Innocent Francis was not some stranger, but rather a faithful servant of the Roman Church who had, in addition, quite a powerful influence among the prelates and dignitaries gathered together at the council. Hence, together with Dominic, Francis could make quite a favorable impression in the eyes of the pope. He would be giving concrete evidence of the success of renewal to those bishops and abbots and religious superiors who had been dragging their feet on committing themselves actively to renew the Church. In fact, already in 1204 the pope had extended an invitation to the abbot of Citeaux (an invitation which he had previously outlined in 1198 in a letter to all the Cistercian abbots) that the monks leave the enclosure of the monastery and organize a mission among the people.

In summary, I do not feel that it is so preposterous an idea to think that the presence of Francis and Dominic together at the council would have been a feather in the hat of the pope in his attempt, amid all his other preoccupations, not to overlook a mighty useful opportunity in convincing others of his quite noble purposes. This does not mean that the two of them were exploited as papal playthings; on the contrary, the pope used their newborn movements with discretion in such a way that would suit a person who, though worried about the current situation, was full of energy and imagination to build the future.

The man was young, and he had no fear of the future. He was just over fifty and had already been pope for seventeen years. No one would have imagined that, shortly after this time, while he was traveling around northern Italy to arrange for transportation by sea for the next crusade, he would die at Perugia. This happened on July 16, 1216.

Near the dying pope in the palace adjoining the cathedral, a little man was there praying. He was one of the penitents, with a tunic and a cord and without any shoes on his feet. His hair was cut in the shape of a crown, the kind of tonsure which clerics wore. It was the dying pope that cut his hair that way the first time when he approved the way of gospel living which he had proposed. Now Francis, through his humble prayer, was thanking the pope for accepting and affirming his proposal. He expressed his thanks by asking Christ the Lord to welcome the Roman Pontiff with open arms, just as the pope had done for him.

The news that Francis was present for the death of Pope Innocent comes to us from Thomas of Eccleston (*Eccleston* 121) who says, when speaking about the death of Innocent IV: "When he died, all of his family abandoned him. But not the Friars Minor. The same thing happened when his predecessors, Gregory, Honorius, and Innocent III, passed away. Even St. Francis himself was present when the latter died...

After his death the pope was clothed in his crimson pontifical regalia, the miter was placed on his head, and his body was placed on the catafalque in the cathedral so that the people could come by and pay their respects. During the night no one thought of keeping vigil besides his mortal remains, or perhaps the people in charge did not carry out their responsibilities. Anyway, robbers took advantage of the situation by stripping the body of its papal finery. What else happened, we do not know. Perhaps the corpse was plundered or violated for reasons of recklessness or maybe even hate. Possibly the body was torn to pieces by, let us hope, some wild animal on the loose. This information, as sketchy as it may be, places us emotionally in the middle of a world so diverse that holiness and brutality, refinement and vulgarity existed side by side in such a way that both were considered absolutely normal.

Jacques de Vitry described the pope's death in the following way: "I left here (Milan) and arrived in Perugia. I found Pope Innocent dead, but not yet buried. During the night some burglars had taken the precious clothes off his dead body, leaving it almost naked and in the state of decay inside the church" (letter written in October of 1216).

On July 18, immediately after Innocent's funeral, the cardinals tried to find a successor. They finally chose Cencio Savelli, who took the name of Honorius III. The new pope was rather old, devout, simple, and gentle. This meekness perhaps turned into a weakness when it came to solving the serious problems which his predecessor had left for him. Particularly the crusade, which had already been announced, was the most pressing problem before him. Part of this concern regarding the crusade was troublesome Emperor Frederick II.

118

Pope Honorius provided the people with a feeling of being protected; he was a good man, he was elderly, he had his feet on the ground. But he was not flexible and imaginative enough to understand the innovative approach that stemmed from Francis' spirit. He understood him even less than could have been expected of Pope Innocent. It was not the people that confounded him; actually, it was the real situation right out there in front of him that he could not comprehend. Francis himself was finding it difficult to be fully aware of the revolution that was burning inside of him. It was much easier for him to intuit what was new than to put it into words, to feel what had to be done than to explain it. The problem was language: he tried but failed to make clear first to himself and then to others what emotions were actually stirring inside that adventuresome spirit of his; it was just inadequate to capture the excitement of his heart.

In that month of July so many things had happened so fast, one after another. First there was the sudden death of Innocent III. Then he was quickly succeeded by electing Pope Honorius, who had to continue the preparation activity for the crusade. And the papal curia was boiling with activity, as can be expected when there is a change of popes.

Francis did not stay in Perugia but headed toward the valley to retire into prayer and meditation at St. Mary of the Angels. The death of that great Pope Innocent gave him a firsthand experience how frail and fleeting human power and human planning really are. He had already experimented with the transitory nature of human glory in quite a personal way, but a temptation stared him in the face: the grandeur and the beauty of being his own private person. With his eyes closed in thought, the loveliness and the sweetness of a wife, a family, and children became so very evident. If all the political designs of a pope can be cut down so quickly to nothing by

119

death, it surely would not be that way with a family and a family line.

The temptation was very human and quite understandable. There was absolutely no reason to be ashamed of it nor to rebel against it. But this also meant that he was tempted to abandon his new way of life in order to grow old as a private person. This he did rebel against, quickly and violently.

Surrounding the place, there was hedge made out of a thicket of brambles which were full of stinging thorns. Francis, without giving it a second thought, threw himself into the thorns to overcome his temptation. It was a crude, medieval solution to upholding an ideal. The brambles had a kind of re-action to the saint's violent action who was now all bloody and in pain. The leaves became tinted with drops of blood, the thorns fell off, and blood-red blossoms opened up.

The legend says that this bed of roses which flowered mi-raculously acted like an intermediary between the temptation of Francis and his prayer at the Porziuncula where he placed himself to beg the Lord to enlighten him and to give him the strength not to abandon the mission he had chosen. His prayer was soon answered because, all of a sudden, a dazzling light invaded the little church, and a vision of paradise ap-peared on the altar. Jesus Christ and the holy Virgin, sur-rounded by angels, asked ·Francis what he desired above ev-erything else at that moment. Francis, who had just overcome his temptation toward selfishness, prayed with a heart full of humility:

"My Lord, though I am a miserable sinner, I ask you to grant your lavish and generous forgiveness, with complete re-mission of all their faults, to whomever comes to visit this lit-tle church in order to repent and confess their sins."

Christ accepted the prayer of his servant through the. inter-cession of the Blessed Virgin Mary, and told him: "Go to my Vicar on earth, the Pope, and request this indulgence on my behalf, so that he can bestow it on all the earth." Francis then went to Pope Honorius who was still in Perugia and told him about the vision and presented him with a wreath of blooming roses.

"For how many years do you want this indulgence?" the pope asked with tenderness. "Holy Father, I am not asking for years. I am asking for souls!"

The pope realized that Francis was asking that the Great Indulgence of the Holy Land be granted to the little unknown church of the Porziuncula. And strangely and unexplainably the pope acceded to his request. But, because of the complaints of the cardinals who had been listening, this concession was limited to one day of the year, the second of August, beginning with First Vespers the evening before.

Francis was overcome with joy because the pope said yes to what he had asked for. When he started to leave while giving thanks to God, the pope called him back and said, "You simpleton! Are you going to leave like this with no document nor any signature?" Francis answered him: "Holy Father, your word is enough for me. I do not need any sort of document. You see, the Virgin Mary wrote the text, Christ notarized it, and the angels witnessed the whole thing." Then, in the presence of the bishops of Umbria, Francis announced the marvelous gift to the people, beginning with these words: "I want to send all of you to heaven!"

The fact of the Porziuncula Indulgence was held under wraps out of fear that it would stir up discontent and would discourage the crusaders from heading off to the Holy Land to get the same indulgence. But after the death of the saint, the news spread quickly, and people by the thousands came from every corner of the world. Even today the same thing happens, as history can readily testify.

The spring of 1217 was just beginning, and with the springtime the followers of Francis began to start walking back from the various places where they had been called to preach and to work to return to St. Mary of the Porziuncula. They came from every part of Italy: the oldest and the youngest, the men well seasoned in this new life and the novices who were eager to meet Francis for the first time having heard so many wonderful things about this person. From north and south they converged on Assisi. Along the way they preached and were credible witnesses, asking only for a bit of bread or for a job, depending on their personal skills or their needs.

The Italians, especially those who lived in the central or northern part of the country, were used to seeing pilgrims, that is, those who headed to Rome to venerate the tombs of the Apostles Peter and Paul. These pilgrims on their way to Assisi, however, were quite different from those on their way to Rome. They carried with themselves no satchels, no leather belts, no wallets, no shoes, not even any horses. There was a procession of Friars Minor heading toward the chapter: that periodic get-together on the plain of St. Mary of the Angels in the center of the valley that stretched from Spoleto on one end to the hills of Perugia on the other. They did not have to be given any particular schedules for arriving or departing, because they had really wanted to come to Assisi. The only set date for everyone, however, was the feast of Pentecost. The calendars of the day were marked more by the liturgical cycle than by days and months.

Pentecost in the year 1217 fell on the fifth of May.

Since his followers were all people without much formal education, even those of the wealthy or noble class, Francis did not have any sort of inferiority complex in talking with them or speaking to them. But as the number of learned and scholarly men began to increase (As we have already seen, Francis received a good number of them along with Thomas of Celano), they started to make him feel somewhat unsure of himself and a bit more afraid.

To tell the truth, this feeling of inferiority was not actually something new to him. For example, he carried around inside of himself those old ambitions to become nobility, even though he kept these desires well hidden under his enthusiasm for the apostolic life he was now living. Nevertheless, these feelings surfaced every once in a while.

A case in point was the time Francis felt compelled to call on Brother Bernard in order to ask him and, in fact, to give him the command to walk over his body and put his foot on the saint's mouth, saying, "Lie there, you country lout, son of Peter Bernardone! How is it that you have so much pride, since you are such an extremely worthless creature?" (*Fior.* 3). This extreme action is something like confessing that one had a "bad thought." He was so discouraged and upset that he was just the son of a merchant without any noble blood flowing through his veins; this feeling of frustration stayed with him because he got tired of constantly trying to get rid of it. I like this story very much because it shows how very human Francis was and at the same time how great a person he was; it is that basic weakness within the human being that causes someone to think and act humbly.

During the chapter Francis' followers would pray together and get to know one another. They met Francis, and they talked about their own experiences, both the good and the bad. They were animated by their high ideals. They were filled with enthusiasm and naturally thought about the future and about what they were going to do. The first thing on the chapter's agenda was to come up with a strategy for preaching, studying various situations and actions in detail. That former restlessness to preach the Gospel to all people, especially to those who had never heard it before, began to surface again. So, they organized their first mission abroad; Brother Giles was sent to the Saracens by way of Tunis, while Brother Elias was sent to Syria.

In this way the friars traveled not just abroad, but overseas.

In all of the commotion throughout the Christian world caused by the crusade, these men from Assisi did not just want to rehash some plan that others had tried, but they were attempting to advance an alternate course of action which would be completely their own. We know that for a long time Francis cherished the idea of going overseas. Twice he tried, and twice be failed. This time with concerted effort he was making a third attempt with two groups. It was going to be a type of "pincer movement": the strategy of the crusades with the agenda of the apostles. It was his goal that the Moslem and Christian brothers, who were only used to having contact through business or through war, should begin a new kind of relationship.

Was there some controversy within the community regarding the mobilization for forces for the crusade? We will never know. We can say, however, that Francis was not a man given to criticism and above all he was not the type of person who would try to second guess anyone, least of all the Roman Church. Even though he was not a critic, he was a person of new ideas. And this was important to him. He was a good-hearted, simple fellow who knew the things which God had revealed to the little ones and had kept hidden from the clever. He threw out new ideas, and opened up new and unexplored horizons without paying much attention to the difficult or complicated consequences which they might find along the way.

So three groups were sent out over the Alps and overseas into the world they really did not know. Francis would stay home alone with his own thoughts. Never before did be come to the point of saying, "Let us get ready, but you set out." This time, that is exactly what he did. And this caused quite a crisis of conscience in him:

"My dearest brothers," he felt the need to say, as he gathered the friars around him, " I ought to be a model and example to all. If I, therefore, have sent my brothers into distant countries where they will undergo fatigue, humiliations, hunger, and all kinds of trials, it is fair and good, it seems to me, that I also leave for a distant country so that my brothers will suffer their trials and privations with patience, knowing that I, too, am enduring as much." As was his custom, he asked the brothers to pray that the Lord would make known to him where it would be best for him to go, and then finally he felt ready to make a decision: "In the name of our Lord Jesus Christ, of the glorious Virgin, his Mother, and of all the saints, I choose the country of France. It is a Catholic nation, and more than all the other Catholic nations of the holy Church, it bears witness to the greatest respect for the Body of our Lord Jesus Christ, and nothing would please me more than to go among these people" (*Leg. Perug.* 79).

Francis set out together with some of his companions, and they traveled in stages, stopping here and there, as would people who tell time not so much by means of a clock but by using a calendar. He stayed over in the towns and villages long enough to preach the Word of the Lord. He did the same thing when he came across the people in the country who were in the process of harvesting during that time. Eventually he arrived at the gate of the city of Arezzo which had fallen prey to a violent internal struggle between opposing factions.

In the Christian tradition such discord was an evident sign of the presence of evil. God is the author of peace; the devil is responsible for all dissension. For this reason Francis started to pray before he decided to enter the city.

In every conflict there are some aspects which can be overcome only by means of a spiritual dimension. Hatred cannot be quenched solely through psychological or sociological solutions. For this reason the first thing the saint wanted to do was to pray that Arezzo would be freed from the power of evil. So he ordered Sylvester, who was a priest, to "command" in the name of God that the demons get out of the city. Sylvester, then, advanced toward the gate and left Francis somewhat behind on his knees. He shouted out in a loud voice, "Praised and blessed be the Lord Jesus Christ. On behalf of God almighty and in virtue of the obedience due to our Father Francis, I order all the devils to leave this city!" (*Leg. Perug.* 81).

Then they went into the city. "Thanks to the goodness of God and the prayer of blessed Francis, it so happened that peace and harmony were restored among the inhabitants of Arezzo without any other kind of sermon." The peace that came about did not happen right away. It was not like some instant, miraculous event. This clearly indicates how, within a religious community, prayer so often serves the purpose of priming the pump in bringing about solutions to the thousands of reasons which cause dissension.

They left Arezzo for Florence. When they arrived, they learned that Cardinal Hugoline of the Counts of Segni was there. The cardinal came from the same family as Innocent III and had come to take a fatherly liking to Francis and his followers. Hugoline was sent to Florence by Honorius III as the pope's representative for Tuscany and Lombardy; this responsibility was confirmed in a papal bull dated January 23, 1217. He was a solid fellow with deep religious convictions. He was fascinated by that whole world of following the Gospel which Francis called forth in people, but at the same time he was quite attuned to the practicalities of life which did not always coincide exactly with the ideal side of life.

Because of the respect the saint had for the cardinal and the affection he felt for him, Francis asked Hugoline if they could meet. Hugoline spoke to him seriously, straightforwardly, and honestly:

"Brother, I do not want you to cross the mountains, for there are a number of prelates and others in the Roman Curia who would like to interfere with the interests of your Order.

Some cardinals and I, who love your Order, will protect it and help it much more effectively if you remain within the frontiers of this province" (*Leg. Perug.* 82).

What he said was quite clear; it came from a man of wisdom and experience who saw in the movement of Francis a religious order so totally new that even its organization was not yet fully developed. Primarily for that reason it needed special attention and care. And he was probably right because Francis' marvelous plan would not have been able to survive the supervision of people who had no imagination nor were used to envisioning concretely the achievable goals which this new way of living was proposing.

When it came down to the practicality of the situation, Francis admitted that the cardinal was right. The vision he had was really like a seed that had to be buried within the soil of the organizational side of religious life, so that it could always be ready to germinate and stir up the winds of renewal when the situation presented itself. One day perhaps his goal of bringing together the Gospel and the world of everyday living would be able to blossom forth from that same earth which simultaneously preserved it and kept it imprisoned. Faced with the cardinal's line of reasoning and with his own reservations, Francis realized that he had to bow to his wishes. At the same time, however, he reiterated a belief that for him was absolutely essential:

"Lord, do you think and believe that the Lord has sent the brothers for this province alone? I say to you in all truth: God has chosen and sent the brothers for the good and salvation of all people in the entire world; they will be received not only in believing countries but also among the infidels. Let them observe what they have promised God and God will give them, both among the infidels and the believing nations, all that they will need" (*Leg. Perug.* 82).

Since he could not go there himself, Francis at least wanted Brother Pacifico and some of the others to continue on their way to France. Meanwhile, he was going to return to the Spoleto Valley. He had made three attempts to leave Italy, and it seemed that God three times said to him, "No! Do not go!" After embarking at Ortona, the first "no" came as a result of the storm. After he tried to go to Spain, the second "no" was caused by physical sickness. Now the third "no" came from the authorities. He felt bound to stay in Italy where all his followers would come together, in order to prevent the death of the movement in its early stages when it needs the most care.

It did not take long for the concerns of Cardinal Hugoline to become the worries of Honorius III. The pope, at that time, grew in his understanding of what position the papacy was to take in regard to the Franciscan movement. In fact, from 1218 onwards, there was a hailstorm of papal decrees to give some parameters to this world of Francis which was growing so rapidly, so strongly, and perhaps so chaotically. Before Pope Honorius no documents written on this topic were ever issued; Pope Innocent only provided oral approvals. He readily gave his counsel and expressed himself in various gestures (like giving Francis the tonsure), but he never put anything in writing. With the first decree of Honorius III – entitled "Cum Dilecti" and dated June 11, 1218 – we find, black on white, the organization of Francis' movement into a clearly structured religious order. The decree straightforwardly warned all people who held positions of authority to regard the followers of Francis as true Catholics who are living a way of life approved by the Church of Rome: "Because my beloved sons, Brother Francis and his companions, have taken on the gospel way of life and are members of the Order of Friars Minor, now that they have left behind the vanities of the world, they have chosen a way of life that is highly approved by the Roman Church. They are expanding into different parts of the world, following the example of the apostles who sowed the seed of the Divine Word. By virtue of this apostolic letter we make known to you our prayer and our exhortation. That is, when the bearers of these letters, who belong to the community of these aforementioned friars, demonstrate the need to travel among you, please welcome them as Catholic and faithful men..."

In this way, Francis' way of life became a focus of attention for the Roman Curia. While he was alive, there were no instances of disagreements or disobedience; but after his death there arose some sensitive times, but they were the exception.

With all of this, Francis started off on a new path. It was not something he found burdensome; on the contrary, he understood it to be necessary. He embraced this new direction not so much as an obligation or restriction, but as the right thing to do (as we have already seen and will continue to see). In accepting all this, however, he will always be trying to point out the yeast which is working underneath the flour and the seed which is germinating underground.

THE WORLD OUTSIDE OF ITALY

I n the year 1219 Pentecost fell on the twenty-sixth of
May.
Like all the other years before, the friars coming from
the most distant locations took to the road right after
Easter in order to arrive on time for the grand reunion in the
Spoleto Valley. Continually new members were joining the
Order and new people were coming from every strata of society. All this rapid growth within and outside of Italy carried
with it a price: their expression of fraternity decreased rather
visibly and their sense of family weakened quite considerably.
At one time in their early history the Porziuncula was the
place to which they returned with eager longing and where
they gathered once again amid so many hugs and "How are
things going?" Now it was becoming more and more the place
where the friars would go to get to know each other, sometimes for the very first time. This might just seem like various
ways to say the same thing, but actually there existed a whole
atmosphere of change. Certainly things could not have been
any more different. By now problems of organization began to
appear and to take over the discussions they used to have
about how great God was and how God had been working
such wonders within everyone and through everybody.

Francis, it is true, made a valiant attempt to keep on being

131

the animating force of the chapter. He tried to strengthen the unity of the groups and to motivate everyone toward a common experience of God and a living expression of fraternity. But, the more he concentrated on being the soul of the movement, the more he was losing control of all that pertained to the body – the tangible events and physical behavior – of the movement. The soul tended to become more sublime while the body was growing more and more faint. What we may describe as a platonic view of reality was showing itself more and more clearly: the soul was viewed as the pilot of the ship; so, even though he was actually guiding that ship, he was not a substantive part of the ship as such. Between the body of the group and its soul, there was beginning to develop that kind of relationship which could be described as two separate and different entities standing side by side.

When the friars filled up every place around the Porziuncula, and they began to pray Evening Prayer for the Vigil of Pentecost, the chapter was solemnly opened. There was an undulating sea of friars in their rough, shaggy habits. There was Francis, overjoyed and lost in thought. And there was Cardinal Hugoline, sometimes one of the group and sometimes standing above the group, cautiously alternating his role within the movement. After all, the presence of a cardinal – with his retinue, horses and knights, processional cross preceding him, and his bright red robes of office – was a sign of their own success and of the attention they were getting from the papal curia over and above the fondness that the person Hugoline was showing them.

The cardinal and Francis stood at an improvised altar in the area out in front of the tiny church. Hugoline celebrated the Eucharist, and Francis chanted the Gospel (he was a deacon). The liturgy unfolded solemnly with its sacred movements, hymns, and quiet prayer. Motivated by the inspiration generated by the penitent of Assisi, Hugoline began to preach his dignified sermon in such a way that he turned dreams into realty. Francis listened to the cardinal and with reverence approved of the message of this man of the Church whom he admired so much and who was for him the kind of loving and caring father which he never pictured Peter Bernadone to be. Even lowering his ideals became acceptable with Hugoline's loving intervention. The cardinal managed to secure Francis' love and trust without damaging the holiness and enthusiasm that pervaded his whole being.

It is true that many historians depict Cardinal Hugoline as a supporter of the monastic tendencies which were soon to appear among the friars. But I do not think that he wanted to betray the aspirations of the saint of Assisi. Perhaps it is correct to say that he was responsible for injecting some "common sense" (in the ways of the world) into the Franciscan Movement; maybe the power of his own personality somewhat tempered Francis' idealism. Nonetheless, he was, first and foremost, a mediator throughout his whole life who made sure that any dangerous rift among the followers of the man of God was avoided.

The chapter ceremonies were over. The friars met with each other and got to know one another. In the tradition of all chapters, they drew some conclusions in 1219 regarding their expeditions over the mountains and across the sea which they had decided to embark upon in the Chapter of 1217. Not everything came off smoothly. The friar missionaries, in public gatherings and private meetings, recalled how absolutely exhausting their journeys were and how difficult it was to find lodging and bread. Languages varied so much, and customs were so different. Not only many of the people but also the clergy did not have a clue what they were talking about. But the fruits of their labors were abundant. They worked hard, but they were successful. The new friars who came from the other side of the Alps agreed to what was being said even though they did not manage to understand everything completely. They also mentioned that they were almost martyred, and this peaked the interest of those listening very much because in those days martyrdom was considered to be a highly prized venture. It was like that period between the nineteenth and twentieth centuries when the well-to-do young men were eager to die for their country as an act of bravery.

Amid their enthusiasm the friars decided, therefore, to send new missionaries off to Germany, France, and Hungary, as well as to Spain which served as a natural bridge to reach Morocco, the land of the Sultan Miramolin (Melek-el-Khamil), to which Francis at one time had tried to go.

When the last of the friars who had come together for the chapter had left the Assisi Valley to set off over the peaks of the Alps or across the sea and to head for Germany, France, Hungary, and Spain, the forest around the Porziuncula became quiet once again. In this silence Francis stayed by himself with his own conscience to think about his own openness to the plans of God. "Some people," he would say from time to time, "are looking for human praise solely because they know how to sing about Roland and the knights of old." He was referring to the minstrels who would travel around to the castles of Italy and France. But now here he was, alone at the Porziuncula, and it seemed to him to be a comfortable shelter to enjoy some leisure time. The others, his companions, were off facing the northern winds and the storms of the sea, while he, their leader, had to stay home to think and observe and wait. Now, if he was the leader, it was proper that he too should put up with the hardships of preaching, just as the others. That old love he had for the lands beyond the sea echoed throughout his soul and his body. With this love came the restlessness for adventure, the dream of being a knight, the zeal of the Christian heart which longs to make contact with

134

the land of Christ. His thoughts passed on to the crusaders' army which at that moment was encamped outside of Damietta. He felt that special love for his Islamic brothers and sisters whom the crusaders were going to fight in battle.

He too decided to leave.

He tightened up his tunic around his sides and went to say good-bye to his brothers and to the image of the Virgin Mary which looked down from above the apse of the Porziuncula. He picked up a stick from the ground and set off walking, ahead of his companions.

This time be did not run into any opposition from the cardinal.

He took the road which led to the Marches. It was on this very road that he, some years before, began his first expedition of evangelization. He walked across the plain almost as far as the gate to the castle of Valfabbrica; then he made his way through the hills and forests which cut off the view of the mountains which are not very high but which divide the territory of Assisi from that of Gualdo. As Francis recounted, he went there with Giles back when there were only four at the Porziuncula and there was more than enough space for them in the chapel. Now the friars at the chapter had to stay outside. Their number had grown so much. How time passes! Not time according to the calendar (barely ten years had gone by), but time in a psychological sense which brings a person to realize deep in the soul how much has completely changed in one's world.

Even today there is a famous legend that makes its way up and down the Italian coast of the Adriatic Sea. It goes like this: very early in the morning of the feastday of St. John the Baptist (June 24), before sunrise, John can be seen taking a bath; his shadow sinks into the sea and comes out again. In this way the saint who baptized Christ and heralded his coming also announces the season of warm weather. At Ortona – which sits on a promontory jutting out into the sea, as if it were trying to stretch toward the East – at daybreak on June 24th, the people still appear on their balconies which stand along the marina in order to catch a glimpse of Saint John taking his bath.

On the morning of June 24, 1219, Francis sailed from Ancona on a crusader ship. The story goes that, in order to choose which among the many friars who wanted to follow him would actually accompany him on the journey, Francis picked a young child to point with his little finger to only eleven of the many who were eager to leave.

Hence, the twelve of them jumped aboard ship heading directly toward the Middle East. Twelve was a good number. It was a bit too big, since they probably did not pay for their passage. And it was a bit symbolic (like the twelve apostles), which gives rise to some doubt about how accurate this information really is. Nonetheless, Francis was at last on his way toward the mission land.

Did he go there for the sake of the crusaders or for the sake of the "Saracens" (Moslems)? Who could ever say what he actually felt deep down in his heart? Probably he went there for the sake of both groups because he would have had something to say to the crusaders and something for the Moslems. Whatever he intended to communicate to the crusaders was immediately clear.

After landing at Akko (which was also known as Acri), he went to Egypt where the Christian soldiers had set up camp in the neighborhood of Damietta which was ruled by the Sultan Melek-el-Khamíl. As soon as he arrived, he started to go against the grain in the manner of the prophet Jeremiah. He predicted their defeat. For this reason he was not liked at all by the army commanders who made no bones about telling him that his pacifist ideas were completely inappropriate. His preaching, however, was very much appreciated by the rank and file of the troops. Some of them arrived on the scene only to leave the army and follow him.

When we speak of the crusades, we should have the good sense to remove from our minds two opposing preconceptions: the first is to consider the crusaders as holy men, abounding with divine grace and filled with good will. This particular bias, in fact, is nothing more than the protection of what those who preached the crusade had dreamed would happen. Some religious figures, like Pope Innocent or Saint Bernard, got locked into propagating such a lovely and neat image, even though it did not correspond to reality.

The other preconception, particularly put forward by people today, views the crusades as a purely worldly-minded effort to achieve new territory, new power, and new markets. We cannot deny that these negative aspects actually existed in abundance. But this is not the whole story.

The reality of the situation is like a field where the weeds are mixed with the grain or like a house where an unabashedly bold person lives right along side a shy and retiring person. From the political point of view, the reality which we are trying to describe is typical of that medieval world of the sacred and the profane. It cannot be interpreted from our categories which separate (or which seemingly presume to separate) what is holy from what is worldly. Whatever the case, Francis simply did not like the crusaders' camp and their methods for "liberating the holy places." His spirit was different not only from that of the merchants who owned the ships and monopolized all the military-commercial traffic organized for the crusade, but also from that of the same church leaders who had dreamed about and preached in favor of and now accompanied the Christians armed against their enemies, the Moslems.

It is safe to say that Francis was not inclined to be part of a protest demonstration. We have already seen, on a number of occasions, that he did not even have the inner "stuff" to be in opposition with someone. He did not know how to be negative, and probably he could not even have managed to see things in a negative way. Francis simply proposed something new for the inside of a person without passing any judgment whatsoever on what might be found on the outside. He never criticized church structures, just as he would never condemn the socio-economic system. He simply kept proposing an alternative. Now, in the crusaders' camp, he operated the same way.

Francis was in the camp, among the tents and the troops. He was even going around prophesying the army's defeats which would follow one after another because of the lack of experience, the lack of preparation, or the lack of military prowess that would make an enemy tremble. It was not that he was criticizing them. He was preaching love and making converts among the soldiers and the clergy. Jacques de Vitry, the author we have already met, who was the archbishop of St. John of Akko at that time, left us some very pertinent information on this point in his letter from Damietta dated February or March of 1220. The inactivity and the failures of the crusaders gave Francis many things to think about and helped him develop some of his plans. He never did believe that a person could secure one's rights by force. That is why he started to think about the most effective ways of removing those fences and walls which divided the two armies.

How could it ever be possible that Christ, who always preached peace, now would want war? And how could it ever be possible that these Moslems were a people – even though they were characterized as strangers and infidels – who were not open to the voice of God, even a little bit? Could they be made to listen to him and to hear the words of the blessed Christ? These thoughts which were racing around in Francis' mind were completely the opposite of the ideas which the common means of communication of that day were conveying regarding the Islamic people and regarding their hatred for the Christian people.

The political climate and the very survival of the name of Christian caused the whole Islamic world to inescapably be turned into demons. This had been going on since the days of the emperor Charlemagne and of the knight Roland. Francis was not even immune from this negative attitude toward Islam. The Legend of Perugia has him saying:

"'The Emperor Charles, Roland, and Oliver, all paladins and valiant knights who were mighty in battle, pursued the infidels even to death, sparing neither toll nor fatigue, and gained a memorial victory for themselves; and by way of conclusion, these holy martyrs died fighting for the Faith of Christ" (*Leg. Perug.* 72).

They were "holy martyrs" first, and only then were they warriors. This was the mentality of the times, and Francis' basic outlook was influenced by it. But it was precisely this cultural perspective that gave rise to his new way of doing things and to his desire to overcome the old point of view; more and more it became a burning conviction inside of Francis and a passionate longing that was born in the depths of his heart.

He so much wanted to cross the crusaders' lines and travel to the Moslem camp. He wanted to talk personally with the sultan. Was this an idea that grew out of some arrangement with an embassy or was it a dream that had pursued him incessantly ever since he arrived? We do not have the arguments to provide an appropriate response to either side; but, already knowing Francis from his psychological makeup, we can readily surmise that he had wanted to go to the sultan from the very first day because he simply did not believe in war.

The pontifical legate immediately gave him permission to go. Maybe it was because he had a lot of respect for Francis. Maybe he just wanted to get rid of this new Jeremiah. Whatever the case and however everything turned out, there was always a positive side to consider: the politico-military outcome of Francis' action could result in something worthwhile; and he could even come out of the whole thing as another martyr who would be praised in the chronicles of the crusade.

Francis set off – poor, barefoot, unpretentious.

The Moslems who were guarding the front line immediately captured him; they caught him because he wanted to be taken. He kept repeating with insistence: "The Sultan! The Sultan!" He fascinated the guards with a captivating but inoffensive demeanor. So, he managed to get himself hauled into the presence of the sultan.

Melek-el-Khamil, as much as is known about him, was a good person with liberal ideas and a tolerant nature. He did not deserve to end up in the middle of a crusade. Unfortunately, this is the way things go. If a person appeared who would have enough good sense to initiate a discussion instead of coming to blows, it would be difficult to find on the other side of the fence another person with the same sort of qualities. On the contrary, it seems that the devil is always bringing opposite sides into conflict. Thus it was with Melek-el-Khamil who had to declare war.

There is a painting by Giotto in the Upper Basilica of St. Francis in Assisi which portrays the Sultan. The portrait was just the fruit of Giotto's imagination, but still, when it is studied, it gives a person enough of a feel for the whole situation. The Moslem pictured by Giotto has a look about him that is much more understanding and congenial than the one who is mounting an assault upon Famagosta.

When Francis came before the sultan, he was so resourceful and animated that the sultan took an immediate liking to him. Since Francis did not know the language, he spoke with gestures (as Italians usually do anyway). He was so spontaneous and absolutely charming. Melek-el-Khamil listened to this short, skinny, little Christian; he took an interest in him and was moved by him. The two of them became friends. He said, "Pray for me, that God may make me understand which is the true religion." It would seem that Francis spoke to him about Christ and about the authenticity of the Christian faith. These were the usual topics taken up when people in those days got together to talk about religion.

There is a certain legend attached to this particular meeting. We are not certain how much of what is told is actually the truth, and we cannot say for sure what language was used to make it possible for the two of them to communicate. Nonetheless, the story talks about how Francis and the wise Moslems were looking for a "proof" from God. Among the paintings of Giotto in the Upper Basilica of St. Francis in Assisi we are able to admire the one already mentioned which represents Francis in the act of passing through the fire as a way of proving that the Christian message is real and true. The impulsive and confident nature of Francis' character would allow us to accept this portrayal as historically accurate. I just know that I myself would not even put my hand in a fire.

The sultan, ultimately, did not want to go through with the test. Neither did his fellow Moslems. The end result of the meeting, however, was the gift of an "oliphant," which can roughly be described as a horn (often from a ram or a bull) used to call people to the hunt or to battle. The songs of the troubadours made the oliphant of the knight Roland quite famous, and this probably stimulated Francis' fantasy about knighthood. We know how much he cherished this precious gift of the horn which, as is recorded, he used for calling the friars together during the chapters.

The calling horn and, likely, the permit of safe passage to visit the holy places of Palestine undisturbed were the only tangible results of this mission. We do not know, however, what psychological and spiritual tokens of their visit Melek-el-Khamil and Francis carried around with themselves in the secret folds of their hearts.

We do find, however, a reference to this point in the sixteenth chapter of the Rule that Francis wrote in 1221, which is known as the "Regula non bullata" (that is, the rule without formal written approbation from the pope) or The Earlier Rule. He talks about those who want to go among the Saracens: "As for the brothers who go, they can live spiritually among [the Saracens and nonbelievers] in two ways. One way is not to engage in arguments or disputes, but to be subject to every human creature for God's sake and to acknowledge that they are Christians. Another way is to proclaim the word of God when they see that it pleases the Lord, so that they believe in the all-powerful God – Father, and Son, and Holy Spirit – the Creator of all, in the Son Who is the Redeemer and Savior, and that they be baptized and become Christians; because whoever has not been born again of water and the Holy Spirit cannot enter into the kingdom of God" (1 *Rule*, 16). These are the same two methods Francis himself had used when he was among the Moslems.

When they separated, the sultan made sure that Francis was shown much respect as he was accompanied back to the crusaders' lines, and they mutually decided to see each other again in the future.

The mission of Francis was a failure for anyone who was expecting that it should have brought about some sort of political solution. The war of attrition dragged on. When finally on the fifth of November the crusaders managed to break through the Moslems' defenses and entered Damietta, they came into a virtual cemetery where, during this extended period of time, starvation and disease killed more people than all of the killings of war.

At one time Damietta was an immense city, but now it was

reduced to a bunch of dead bodies among which were wandering only a few thousand people. The spectacle was absolutely disgusting, and not for a single moment could the man of God enjoy the triumph of the crusaders. Who would call it a victory?

Nonetheless, from a military point of view, this conquest was not to be underrated. The city was surrounded by a double circle of walls on the side that overlooked the coast and by a triple circle on the side guarding the mainland. It had twenty-two gates, 110 towers, and forty-two fortifications. It was protected by a strong garrison and was supplied with enough provisions to last for two years.

As far as he was able, Francis expressed his strong opposition to this slaughter. The people thought he was crazy, which was to be expected. He was unable to convert the Moslems and his words fell on deaf ears among the Christians. So, he returned to Syria where his minister Brother Elias was. He intended to visit the holy places, and he probably did just that.

Meanwhile, the other expeditions which the chapter decided would be initiated outside of Italy were being carried out. Jordan of Giano, who had been sent to Germany by Francis, provides this most animated report:

"When the brothers who went to France were asked if they were Albigenses, they answered that they did not know who the Albigenses were; and so, being ignorant of the fact that the Albigenses were heretics, they themselves were put down for heretics. But when the bishop and the masters read their Rule and saw that it was truly in accordance with the Gospel and Catholic, they took counsel about the matter with the lord Pope Honorius. The Pope, however, declared in a letter that the Rule was authentic, since it had been confirmed by the Holy See, and that the brothers were in a very special way sons of the Roman Church and true Catholics. He thus freed them from the suspicion of heresy.

"Sent to Germany, however, was Brother John of Penna with some sixty or more other brothers. These, when they came to Germany and, being ignorant of the language, were asked if they wished to be sheltered or to eat, or the like, answered "ja"; they were accordingly treated kindly by some of the people. And seeing that because of this word "ja" they were treated kindly, they resolved to answer "ja" to whatever question they would be asked. Whence it happened that when they were asked if they were heretics and if they had come to corrupt Germany as they had corrupted Lombardy and they replied "ja", some of them were cast into prison, others were stripped and led naked to a dance and made a ludicrous spectacle before their fellowmen. The brothers, therefore, seeing that they would not be able to gather a harvest in Germany, returned to Italy. As a result of these things, Germany had a reputation among the brothers of being so cruel that they would not dare to return there unless they were filled with a desire for martyrdom.

"The brothers, however, who were sent to Hungary were conducted there by sea by a certain bishop from Hungary. And as they walked through the fields, they were derided, and the shepherds sent their dogs upon them and kept striking them with their staves, the point, however, being turned away. And when the brothers debated among themselves why they were being treated like this, one said: 'Perhaps because they wish to have our outer tunics.' But when they had given them these, they did not cease their blows. He added: 'Perhaps they wish to have our under tunics also.' But when they had given them these, they did not leave off their blows. He then said: 'Perhaps they want our breeches too.' When they gave them these, they stopped their blows and let them go away naked. One of these brothers told me that he had lost his breeches fifteen times in this way. And since, overcome by

144

shame and modesty, be regretted losing his breeches more than his other clothing, he soiled the breeches with the dung of oxen and other filth, and thus the shepherds themselves were filled with nausea and allowed him to keep his breeches. These brothers, afflicted with other insults too, returned to Italy" (Jordan of Giano, 4-6).

Six of them had set out for Spain on their way to Morocco. A severe illness prevented Vitale, the leader of the group, from continuing on the journey, but he gave the other five permission to go on without him. The group soon reached Moslem country. In spite of all good intentions, they behaved in such a way that they instigated all sorts of conflict. They completely lacked any tact, and roused the anger of the people and of the local authorities when they preached about Jesus Christ and talked against Mohammed. More than once they were asked not to over-state their case so that they would not do damage to the very profitable commercial activity that was going on between the Christians and the Moslems. But, deaf to these pleadings and warnings, they insisted on carrying on. As it happens, the day of doom arrived. The Moslems could not put up with any more; with fury they slaughtered the friars.

We now venerate them as holy martyrs, but we cannot honestly blame the Moslems for their fierce anger. They lost their temper when they heard them preach against Mohammed, even inside of the mosque. Their names are Berard, Peter, Accursius, Adjutus, and Otto. They were decapitated on January 16, 1220. Their remains were transported to Coimbra, Portugal. On this occasion the Augustinian canon Fernando was overcome with the idea of being a missionary. He left his Order and became a Friar Minor, taking the name of Anthony. Today we venerate him as St. Anthony of Padua.

When Francis became aware of their martyrdom, he cried

out full of emotion: "Now we can say that finally we have five Friars Minor!" Pope Sixtus IV canonized the five of them in 1481.

In the spring of 1220, when the storms calmed down, Francis was looking for a ship to carry him back to his homeland when he received the alarming news about the situation in Italy. Now we will take a look at what was going on.

STRUCTURE AND INSPIRATION

J acques de Vitry, whom we have already come across as a witness to the events which took place within the papal court in 1216 – that is, when Pope Innocent died and Honorius succeeded him – was in the crusaders' camp when Francis got there. Today we still have one of his letters describing the taking of Damietta. It was written there in 1220 and was addressed, most likely in triplicate, to Pope Honorius, to Master John of Nivella and to the abbess of the monastery of Aywieres.

The letter confirms his understanding of and support – which did not come cheaply – for the movement from Assisi. In fact, he wrote: "Colin, our cleric from England, and two of our co-workers, namely, Master Michael and Lord Matthew (to whom I had entrusted the care of the Church of the Holy Cross) now have become members of this religious Order. With difficulty I am managing to hold back the cantor [John of Cambrai], Henry [the administrator of the estate], and a few others..."

A man who can lose his servants and friends without any resentment, while at the same time keeping alive his feelings of support and affection, is a reliable person. We can trust him even when he critiques the newly developing Order. While remarking how fast the Friars Minor were growing in number, he stressed a certain lack of adequate training among the new members: "It seems to us that this religious order is involved in something very seriously dangerous, for not only are the perfect being sent two by two throughout the world, but also men who are too young and immature and who should be kept under control and tested for some time under the discipline of community life."

In regard to the issue of likening the movement to an order, 1220 is the year of truth. It was during this year that Pope Honorius, as we shall see in more detail later on, imposed a period of novitiate upon the friars as a precondition for religious profession. Thus the movement of Francis had landed at a secure point. Everybody now was able to give it a name and give it a place within the structures of the Church without any fear of wondering where it belonged. Structure – any structure – provides a certain level of confidence and relieves the anxiety of those who are afraid of what may happen when the impetuous aspects of human nature are not kept under control. A herd of wild horses on a rampage frightens those who get too close. Marshalling those who guard the horses provides security; and any old, tottering president whatsoever would be able to pass by them in review.

But what was the reason that brought about this intervention on the part of the pope?

For an answer, we have to refer back to history. As we have just seen, Francis, in the autumn of 1219, had embarked for the Holy Land, not following the crusaders immediately, but coming somewhat later upon the wake of their travels. During this long time away, things began to happen in Italy among his various followers. These were happenings that caused a lot of anxiety. Cardinal Hugoline had been right when, in May of 1217, he had tried to prevent Francis from leaving the country. He used all his skill and all his authority to convince him.

But in the end Francis left without the cardinal blocking the way.

His followers conspicuously missed him very much as a point of reference in their lives, and they began to find themselves falling apart without him.

Actually, Francis left in Italy two friars as vicars to take his place: a certain Matthew of Narni and Brother Gregory of Naples. Very little, if anything, is known about the first one. The second, on the other hand, had his share of arguments within the Order in years to come, till in 1239 when the general chapter actually ordered him to be incarcerated. Matthew's responsibility was to stay at the Porziuncula, to oversee the formation of the new people coming in, and to represent a stable and hence easily approachable authority. The other vicar, Gregory, was to travel around to the various places where the friars lived in order to encourage life in fraternity.

As I have pointed out more than once, Francis' revolutionary charism during this period of time was trying to stay alive amid all the difficult repercussions of the situation at hand and of the people who were able to be stirred up by his example but were not able to understand a reality that was not organized and classified according to the categories of the preexisting models of religious life, namely, the monastic orders. This is why Francis' short absence, plus the authority left in the hands of his two vicars, was enough to cause the unsteady balance which existed to dizzily plummet toward a cloistered and monastic expression of the Franciscan ideal.

Friar Jordan of Giano, in the first pages of his Chronicle, related that the two vicars, with the support of the most authoritative friars, called the Chapter at Pentecost of 1220 to legislate the matters of fasting and abstinence in a way that was more strict and precise than what was found in the "way of life" (this is the "rule" which would have been very similar to what was originally presented to Pope Innocent back in

1209). This need to regulate fasting with a new austerity seems to us now to be a matter of splitting hairs, but that was not the case in those days.

Behind the obligation to fast and abstain was all the stuff involved in a trend to promote and revive monastic life which was quite prevalent at that time because it carried with it the consequence of a peaceful economic existence dedicated to the possibility of owning property sooner or later. As is evident, Francis was away from Assisi for just a few months, and already a great chasm was cleft between the various groups of his followers. With him being absent, he could not make his voice and his authority felt. In a sense, it was as though he had died and left the way wide open for so many attempts to pull in the reins and make things more strict because of the quality of vocations or because of mental laziness. All the more did this seem so because rumors were circulating that the man of God had probably died in the Middle East.

But somebody did not like how things were going in Italy; that person tried his utmost. He took a copy of the old rule and a parchment with the new norms and set off for the Orient into the land of the Saracens. (He probably had help in pulling this off because of some connection with a crusader.) And he joined Francis.

The first thing he did was to ask pardon for his disobedience. He left Italy without the permission of the vicars, and this, especially in virtue of the situation which was becoming more and more prevalent, was one of the most serious infractions he could have done. When structures tend to close in upon themselves, then any way of striking out individually at those in charge becomes a threat to the whole organization. Sometimes, though, structures can work the other way by allowing the individual person enough room to develop one's own talents and gifts.

So, the friar asked for pardon and then started jabbering

without stopping, saying to Francis: "Your two vicars have called a chapter at St. Mary of the Angels and have imposed on us new rules for fast and abstinence. From now on we have to fast on Mondays, Tuesdays, and Thursdays, over and above what we are already doing on Wednesdays and Fridays. On Mondays and Saturdays, moreover, we are not allowed to take any dairy products."

Francis and his companion Friar Peter, meanwhile, were sitting at table and had before them a nice plate of meat. In such cases the easiest thing to do would be to strictly abide by the law. Francis, however, had inculcated into his disciples the notion of being responsible for making their own decisions and of taking the risk of figuring out what is permissive and what is not, when there were not any precise commandments from God nor any definite teachings of the Church. Contrary to what people usually think, this is not an easy thing to do. In this uncomfortable situation, Francis took the trouble to make the decision. Either he could go by the decision by the friar and obey what the chapter legitimately decreed in his absence, or else he should conform to his former astute idea of the freedom of the children of God in observing the holy Gospel. So he asked Friar Peter Catanii: "Sir Peter, now what are we going to do?" Francis had a great admiration for Friar Peter because he was an educated man with a noble bearing. That is why he addressed him with the title "sir," one which tells us quite a bit about the inner thoughts and feelings of a person in love with the world of nobility minus its fascination with riches and its preoccupation with power.

"We will do what pleases you, Sir Francis," replied Peter, who was always ready to obey. Already the meat was getting cold because their indecision was delaying their eating.

"Come on now," Francis stated, "the Gospel comes before the chapter held at the Porziuncula. Let us eat what we have before us, as the Lord commands in the Gospel of St. Luke!"

And with peace of heart they ate the meat on that day which the friars had designated as a day of abstinence.

This episode, though it is a simple story to tell, is quite profound in its meaning. Once again it shows how wrong those biographers of Francis were who had envisioned his way of life being organized into some great detailed ascetic project of vices and virtues without the intervention of that rich human touch which characterized Francis' personality It would be impossible to categorize this episode under either an example of the virtue of obedience or an act of penance. The fact of the matter is that we do not find this story in the earliest official biographies of the saint. The matter of the meat was resolved in a very simple way, but Francis was really alarmed. What was actually happening in Italy? He was needed there, and it was not very wise at all for him to leave his own country and travel around Palestine.

He went to the harbor and waited for the next ship to Italy. He begged the crew to let him come aboard, for the love of God. On this journey home he was accompanied by Peter Catanii and Elias (the one who, as result of the Chapter of 1217, was sent to Syria as the minister for the countries overseas). Also there was Caesar of Speyer whom Francis held in high regard because of his deep knowledge of the Sacred Scriptures. The qualifications and characteristics of these three companions who he took back to Italy with him shows how thoroughly he was preoccupied with this matter.

The ship disembarked at Venice.

Once be got to Italy – it was mid-summer of 1220 – Francis went about inquiring about the present situation, but he avoided coming in contact with the more representative members of the group which had orchestrated the direction of the Pentecost Chapter. From Venice he went back onto the Italian Peninsula and traveled to Rome to seek advice, affirmation, and assurance. If his movement really had to turn into an organized religious order, at least he should do it within the Catholic Church under the authority and guidance of the pope. He had gone to the pope to ask permission for his great dream. This time he looked for the pope's okay to give shape to what was left of that proposal which in 1209 he had shared with Innocent III. Whether he is named Innocent or Honorius, Francis, ultimately, always turns to the pope.

FROM MINISTER GENERAL TO CONTEMPLATIVE

I t was late in the summer. The Venetian hills and the plains which followed were beautiful and rich with vegetation. The valleys and hills did not look anything like this in Palestine and Egypt. Francis was looking at his native Italian countryside once again. And though the uncertainty about the future was a bitter pill to swallow, the fields around him made the journey much more pleasant.

As he slowly moved from Venice toward the south, the amount of information increased, and the friars who happened to be living in places near where he passed reacted in many different ways to his return. What was Francis going to do next?

The friars were divided in their opinion: some were still dreaming of the good old days when they felt free and happy, content only to preach the Gospel. Others – friars who were wiser and more prudent and perhaps even more educated – preferred the prose of juridical norms to the poetry of adventure. They probably could justify their position by saying that official, strict, monastic-like norms would surely put a stop to so many cases of irresponsible and libertine behavior rampant among the friars. Francis shared the dream of the first group and tried to take into account what motivated the others.

After a short time he was in the vicinity of Bologna. It was the city of towers, the university city, the city of wise and educated people. With every step that brought him nearer to the city, a combination of attraction and aversion churned inside of him and increased in intensity.

He had good memories of Bologna. It was here that he came to know how learning could become the friend of simplicity. He had experienced this when the warmth of unrefined speech touched the hearts of many wise professors, who eventually became penitents like him, embracing a life of humility and devotion. Would he still find that same sort of thing? What could he have said – he who felt so uneducated – to those people who knew so much about law and theology, about rhetoric and Latin?

When he entered the city, he asked where the friars lived. They showed him. It was a building of stone and mortar with a solid roof and strong doors and windows. This was not the place he had left! It was a bitter pill for Francis to swallow.

Using his imagination to picture something like scenes from a movie, he saw himself as head of the household, giving orders, directing people about, taking charge, like an abbot. Using his mind, he gave shape to some thoughts that had been rumbling around in his head for a while. It was something he wanted to communicate to the friars. Shortly thereafter he would write:

"None of the brothers should be administrators or managers in whatever places they are staying among others to serve or to work, nor should they be supervisors in the houses in which they serve. ...The brothers should be aware that, whether they are in hermitages or in other places, they do not make any place their own or contend with anyone about it" (1 *Rule* 7:1,13).

"They do not make any place their own"; and he indeed did not have one. He paid rent to the Benedictine monks for the Porziuncula.

"They do not contend with anyone about it"; now for sure he was remembering the episode of the farmer of Rivotorto who by giving the donkey a good push, had evicted him and his first companions from that hovel.

He so much wanted to enter the house and meet his fellow friars; he was so anxious to see them again. The ideal he had to stand up for was stronger than his feelings. So, he passed by the building. He turned his back on the place where the friars lived; sadly he set off toward the city gate and left.

He hesitated for a brief moment, and then, in a outburst of defiance, he stopped suddenly and ordered one of the companions who was with him to turn around and serve an eviction notice to the friars living within the stone building. The house occupied by the friars was an insult to poverty and a betrayal of their original enthusiasm. He was so determined on this point that he would have forced even a sick friar to get out.

That command – so unexpected, so decisive – set everybody in an uproar. Francis returned from the East with renewed determination, and he began to strike back by beginning right there at that place where the most scholarly friars were concentrated, those who were intent upon pursuing their studies in the peace and quiet of their house.

This action marked the beginning of a crisis with wide ramifications. By now there were thousands of friars and, if it were not so in theory, certainly in practice, they were in the beginning stages of a very large religious order which really needed the organization and the milieu which all the other religious communities had. Humanly speaking, the mode of operation which was found at St. Mary of the Angels among the early penitents was just no longer viable.

Cardinal Hugoline, however, happened to be in Bologna. The friars who were evicted had recourse to him because they knew he would act wisely and compassionately toward the followers of the penitent from Assisi. They also knew him as a person who, while appreciating Francis' impulsive nature, was able to inject a certain amount of prudence into his decisions so that the whole thing did not get ruined.

The cardinal met their expectations very well. He found the way to resolve the whole situation by using his talent for compromise and attentiveness and by offering some reasons based on solid and honest good sense. He told Francis not to have any fear whatsoever regarding poverty, because he himself would take on the public ownership of the house, and the friars would stay there as his guests. Necessity and opportunity quieted Francis down. One by one, the friars moved back into the rooms they had abandoned. The organizational control of Cardinal Hugoline moved ahead slowly, prudently, and without any traumatic splits.

Absolute poverty – that is, not possessing anything, even a place to lay one's head, as Jesus said in the Gospel – turned out to be practically impossible for a movement which by now was certainly becoming an institution. By this time the certainty of having a center was just as psychologically important as the assurance of having detailed norms for living to put some order into their everyday existence.

So, they arrived at a compromise: the friars would stay at places for which they did not hold the title of ownership. This so-called "nominal possession" (or ownership in name only) still exists today because technically the Holy See holds the title of ownership for whatever the friars have. In this way poverty was salvaged in principle.

As for the detailed rules and regulations for everyday living which put a crimp on the ideal of freedom, a new solution was reached: a short and open-ended rule, which down through the centuries would be followed by a plethora of "constitutions" and "statutes." Such documents would be aimed at stemming any sense of uncertainty and fear which people who are not seasoned in this way of life always feel when face to face with the real possibility of personal liberty.

The Bologna episode introduces in no uncertain terms the figure of the aging Cardinal Hugoline right into the middle of all what Francis was undertaking. He comes upon the scene as a wise man who felt a sincere friendship for Francis and the friars. Perhaps never before had two men of such different temperaments been able to get along so well. Their mutual esteem and trust grew out of their awareness of that intense honesty and openness which they shared with each other. Hugoline viewed Francis as a holy man. Francis – as his biographers, his companions, and even Hugoline himself indirectly all attest – saw prophetically in the cardinal the future Pope Gregory IX; and he always treated him as such.

After Bologna, Francis set out for Rome. It was a bittersweet experience for him to pass through all the places where his friars lived as he traveled along toward the Eternal City; he enjoyed seeing the friars again, but he keenly felt the pain of coming to terms with so many things that had fallen apart because of his absence. He, however, was too clever not to understand the heart of the matter. If his brief absence – combined with the rumors that he had died could have brought about so many unpleasant changes, this meant that this was the way it was supposed to be. It was no use fighting against destiny!

So, as he walked along the roads and moved through the forests where he stopped to pray quietly as he journeyed slowly toward Rome, he began to develop in his mind the opinions and decisions he would have to make to turn his movement into a true religious order. One, though, that had a totally unique look to it and contained within it an immense amount of a leavening agent, strong enough to induce at a moment's notice some unexpected fermentation.

Francis understood. The fire which was ignited and which burned brightly in those early years now began to give off less heat and more smoke. The growing number of followers was to the detriment of quality. The ideal of freedom, which can only be experienced by people who are mature and which he had always dreamed about, was now threatening to turn itself into harmful spontaneity. Sooner or later, Francis thought to himself, I am going to find myself among people of folly and defiance who eventually will end up, like so many others, in the position of rebellion and even heresy. His opinion was backed up with some evidence, as is noted by Jordan of Giano:

"Brother Philip, who was over-zealous for the Poor Ladies [that is, the nuns of St. Clare], contrary to the will of Blessed Francis who wanted to conquer all things through humility rather than by the force of legal judgments, sought letters from the Apostolic See. By these letters he wished to defend the Ladies and excommunicate their disturbers. Similarly, Brother John from Campello, after he had gathered together a large crowd of lepers, both men and women, withdrew from the Order and wanted to be the founder of a new Order. He wrote a Rule and presented himself with his followers before the Holy See to have it confirmed. And in addition to these things there were rumblings of other disturbances too that had arisen during the absence of Blessed Francis" (*Jordan of Giano*, 13).

As disturbing and as hurtful as this was, it was really happening. To confront the situation, Francis had absolutely no doubt as to what he had to do (it was deeply rooted in his soul!): he chose the Roman Church. He simply could not cope with the thought that the movement which he was able to start up would in any way drift away from the Church. And it was preferable for the movement to suffer the risk of losing its originality and novelty than losing its Catholic character. This was a hard decision to make. But Francis' ideas were very clear in this regard, and he was not willing to compromise on this point. For him the Church is the living Body of Christ and not an institution. He said, in fact:

"I will go and entrust the Order of Friars Minor to the holy Roman Church. The rod of her authority will daunt and retrain those who wish it ill, and the sons of God will everywhere enjoy full freedom to pursue their eternal salvation. Let her sons acknowledge the kindly blessings of their Mother, and embrace her sacred feet with particular devotion.

"Under her protection no harm will come upon the Order, and the son of Satan will not trample over the vineyard of the Lord with impunity. Our holy Mother will herself imitate the glory of our poverty, and will not permit our observance of humility to be overshadowed by the cloud of pride. She will preserve unimpaired the bonds of love and peace that exist between us, and will impose her gravest censure on the unruly. The sacred observance of evangelical poverty will ever flourish before her, and she will never allow the fragrance of our good name and holy life to be destroyed" (*Spec. Perf. 78*).

Francis met the pope even, before arriving in Rome, because during that time he was staying at Orvieto. With this decision in his heart and with the bitter taste in his mouth that he was brought to the point of choosing between two things that he loved, he climbed the limestone rocks to Orvieto. The summer heat was intense, and the city streets were filled with dust. As he traveled along the long road built with human energy and enterprise, he put behind him those past experiences of the human condition: wickedness, impulsive behavior, depravity, hate and doubt. The teeming confusion of the crusaders' camp, the friendship with the sultan, the bloody slaughter of Damietta, the encounter with people of a different faith, the return to Italy, the disappointments – all these things were still alive in Francis' mind and heart. His skinny little figure seemed even smaller now under the burden of his dreams and disillusionments.

He looked around for Cardinal Hugoline who could arrange for him an audience with the pope. In fact, it turned out to be more than that. Right away the cardinal gave him the chance to address the pope in a full consistory, that is, an official meeting with all of the available cardinals present. The occasion was very special. The various cardinals who had heard so many people talking about Francis were very eager to get to know this fellow, to listen to what he had to say, to give their own estimation of what he was up to. Cardinal Hugoline felt that Francis' credibility and, perhaps even a bit of his very own, was at stake at this consistory. Envy and rivalry were not completely left outside the door. Francis appeared at this solemn event barefoot and wearing a straight tunic, which gave the impression that he was even thinner than he actually was. But it was clear that he was not intimidated at all by the papal court.

He began to speak. He came out of experiences so very different from those of the members of the court. He possessed an inner world that was so very rich. He talked about God and about the testimony needed to be given to him. Cardinal Hugoline was all ears. He experienced a deep inner joy, and at the same time, he was afraid that the unpredictability of human nature would take hold of the saint and cause him to say or do something he would sorely regret later. While Francis spoke, he was very tense and he prayed that everything would go well. Francis had intended to talk about his own situation, but right away he was taken up with talking about God who must be loved and recognized as good, all good, the highest good, because God alone is good.

Indeed, he spoke with such great fervor of spirit, that, not being able to contain himself for joy, when he spoke the words with his mouth, he moved his feet as though he were dancing, not indeed lustfully, but as one burning with the fire of divine love, not provoking laughter, but drawing forth tears of grief. For many of them were pierced to the heart in admiration of divine grace and of such great constancy in man" (*1 Cel 73*).

He had passed the test of the pontifical court and of the pope himself, but he forgot to mention anything about the questions dealing with his Order, which is why he came there in the first place. The next day, or some days later, he realized that he still needed to speak to the Supreme Pontiff. So, he went to the palace where, afraid that he might be a nuisance, he waited humbly in the antechamber for a chance to meet the pope. He awaited his turn to ask whether he could speak with him, just as any other poor petitioner would have done. When the pope came out, Francis greeted him with the words, "O Father Pope, may God give you peace!" "And may God bless you, my son," the pope replied. Francis then said to him: "Behold, I know that you are so very busy, but I need to resolve the many problems of my Order. I certainly cannot come to you every time. So, please, appoint someone for me who can act in your stead as a delegate instead of the many people who now are taken up with the concerns of my friars. Many things will be able to be settled more readily if only one person is in charge".

Pope Honorius satisfied his request, and Cardinal Hugoline was given full authority to intervene without restrictions whenever it was necessary, thus continuing the work he had begun quite a while ago with his friends, the Friars Minor.

His task was to form a body which would receive its spirit from the project for living which Francis set forth.

This is why, in the Order of Friars Minor, the spirit of the founder extends itself a lot farther than the actual body of friars.

Francis called Hugoline his own "pope" and he no longer

felt alone in facing the future which down the road did not seem overly happy. He worried over the decline of dedication, and this caused a lot of suffering for him which actually turned into discouragement. He knew human nature quite well, and he quickly realized that his feelings of being disheartened were not all "pure". In other words, maybe there was some wounded self-love or a bit of hurt pride or a subtle attempt to "embezzle" something which was not his but which really belonged to God.

The Legend of Perugia (86) recounts the following story, which Thomas of Celano, St. Bonaventure, and the Mirror of Perfection all corroborate:

"One day, noticing and learning that certain ones were giving bad example in the order and that the brothers were not maintaining themselves on the heights of their profession, Francis was painfully moved to the depths of his heart and said to the Lord in his prayer: 'Lord, I give you back the family you gave me.' The Lord answered him: 'Tell me, why are you so sad when a brother leaves the Order or when others do not walk in the way I have shown you? Tell me, who planted the Order of the brothers? Who converts men and urges them to enter it to do penance? Who gives them the strength to persevere? Is it not I?' And the inner voice said to him: 'In you I did not choose a scholar nor an orator to govern my religious family, but I wanted a simple man so that you and the others may know that I am the one who watches over my flock.'"

Francis captured the meaning of what the Lord was saying as though it were a psalm refrain. The Lord was suggesting to him to be more detached without carrying the burden of giving good example always and everywhere. As was his custom, he took this to prayer and quickly came up with a decision: he would no longer carry the responsibility of ruling the Order as its superior. Besides, the Order now had the wise and attentive presence of Cardinal Hugoline.

As a result of this thought process, he decided to resign as minister general. He would do so in order that he could act as a leaven within the community. So, this is what he announced: "As of today and as far as you are concerned, I am dead. But here is Brother Peter Catanii whom all of us will obey" (*Leg. Perug.* 105).

And from then on he would often repeat to his friars: "I resolved and swore to observe the rule; the brothers are also pledged to do so. Since I resigned my post as superior because of my sickness, for the greatest good of my soul and of my brothers, my only obligation to them is to give them good example" (*Leg. Perug.* 87).

The sickness he mentioned was partly real and partly a diplomatic ploy: "I relinquished my post and resigned, excusing myself at the general chapter because my sickness would not allow me to care for the brothers. And yet, if the brothers had walked and were still walking according to my will, I would prefer that they have no other minister but myself until the day of my death" (*Leg. Perug.* 76).

Francis' resignation was not an attempt to escape. Rather, it was the awareness that he could no longer cope with the amount of attention and work required to organize and maintain the community and to provide discipline for so large a number of persons. It was his wish that his exhortations and his example would be enough to guarantee the spiritual wellbeing of all of his followers. Since this did not work, he said: "I cannot turn myself into a torturer who hits and whips those who are guilty, as do the temporal rulers of this world." As we can see, Francis was right in the middle of that never-ending debate between the spirit and the letter which St. Paul writes about. This situation creates a constant tension within the Church of Christ which exists within the framework of time but which can never be subjected to just the exigencies of time.

ROOTS AND WINGS

After he resigned his responsibilities as minister general, Francis had more time to dedicate to prayer, contemplation, and good example. He did not rule with the authority of a superior, but instead he did provide real leadership as guide and inspiration. He did not have all those practical problems to resolve as an official leader, yet he very much remained in charge of setting the direction for the future.

Now in his memory and in real life he could return to living those wonderful moments when he first started off, when he got his first companions, when he witnessed the development of the primitive community. With the new friars, who were so young and always so eager to search him out whether he was fasting on Mount Subasio or praying in the fissures of the caves at Sant'Urbano, Francis used to share with nostalgia the "olden days" of his experience.

"He used to say that a good Friar Minor should imitate the lives and possess the merits of these holy friars: the perfect faith and love of poverty of Brother Bernard; the simplicity and purity of Brother Leo, who was a man of most holy purity; the courtesy of Brother Angelo, who was the first nobleman to enter the Order and was endowed with all courtesy and kindness; the gracious look and natural good sense of

Brother Masseo, together with his noble and devout eloquence; the mind upraised to God, possessed in its highest perfection by Brother Giles; the virtuous and constant prayer of Brother Rufino, who prayed without ceasing, and whose mind was ever fixed on God, whether sleeping or working; the patience of Brother Juniper, who attained the state of perfect patience because be kept the truth of his low estate constantly in mind whose supreme desire was to follow Christ on the way of the Cross; the bodily and spiritual courage of Brother John of Lauds, who in his time had been physically stronger than all men; the charity of Brother Roger, whose whole. life and conversation was inspired by fervent charity; the caution of Brother Lucidus, who was unwilling to remain in any place longer than a month, for when he began to like a place, he would at once leave it, saying, 'Our home is not here but in heaven'" (*Spec. Perf.* 85).

He retired from office in order to communicate with more freedom the experience of being a religious person, and we have evidence of this work of his in the thousands of stories which the friars passed on to one another about him during their spiritual gatherings. In fact, even though many of the friars wanted to know all the gossip and acted like busybodies, still they were men of deep spirituality. By then the Order was already beginning to face the dichotomy which would later be a characteristic feature. On one side of the ledger, the Order was seen as a large, organized, powerful, and disciplined movement; on the other, one with people so enthused about the spiritual life but less efficient than before and more inclined toward devotion. So many anecdotes, witty remarks, and stories flourished:

"How Francis admonished a friar when he was sad." "How he taught the friars how to satisfy bodily need with the practice of prayer." "How the devil got into the pillow that the saint had under his head." "How Francis had a premonition of the profound temptation of another friar." "Regarding the extraordinary love he felt for the birds called hooded larks because they reminded him of a good religious." "Regarding his very special love for water, stones, trees, and flowers." "How he spoke against hypocrites." "How be gave away his cloak to someone who was even poorer than he was." And so forth.

The stories and the anecdotes and the legends just kept growing and growing. The older friars kept sharing their memories with the younger friars, and they would pass them on among themselves, as was the practice of a peasant society where people would gather around the fire in winter or would work together on the threshing floor in summer in order to have the chance to talk and tell stories and sing songs.

Meanwhile, the days and the months passed by. The countryside became barren, and the bare feet of the friars started to get cold during those long vigils of prayer throughout the night. During the winter there was not always work for the friars who willingly set off to seek employment in order to get a piece of bread or a handful of beans. They felt like the birds which could not find anything to eat. So they had to go out begging with the hope that someone would give them a bit of bread or a fistful of chickpeas or garbanzo beans. When Christmas arrived, they really felt the psychological need of having something more than they usually had day in and day out. One day Francis had a dream; he heard a voice from on high, and he thought about his friars scattered all over the world knocking at the back doors of the peasants and the rich alike. Here is what he said:

"If I ever speak to the Emperor, I shall beg him for love of God and myself to enact a special law, forbidding anyone to kill our sisters the larks or do them any harm. Similarly, all mayors of towns and lords of castles and villages should be obliged each year on the Nativity of our Lord to see that their people scatter wheat and other grain on the roads outside the towns and villages, so that our sisters the larks and other birds may have food on such a solemn festival. And in reverence for the Son of God, Who with the most blessed Virgin Mary rested in a manger that night between an ox and an ass, anyone who owns an ox or an ass should be obliged to give them the choicest of fodder on Christmas Eve. And on Christmas Day the rich should give an abundance of good things to all the poor" (*Spec. Perf.* 114).

Christmas of 1220 was over. The cold and snow were gone, the air was warming up, and the fields of Umbria were alive with the spring colors of new greenery and plants.

But with the sun and with the springtime came another event at St. Mary of the Porziuncula: the death of Peter Catanii, the saintly man whom Francis himself chose as his vicar when he gave up the governance of the Order. Today the remains of Brother Peter still rest at the Porziuncula. On the wall of the tiny church there's an ancient inscription on stone which has been rubbed smooth and shiny by the millions of hands that have touched it; it continues to remind us of him and to ask the Lord to bless him. After Peter's death the Order required Francis' active presence all the more.

Meanwhile, the resignation of Francis as minister general and the sudden death of his vicar caused throughout the fraternity an understandable feeling that things were coming apart. How much longer was Francis going to live? What was going to happen to the Order after the death of Peter Catanii? These two questions were sufficient to explain why so many friars – about 5,000! came together for the Pentecost Chapter of 1221. There were so many of them that the memory of all the other chapters that went before it paled into insignificance.

Five thousand friars! The plain of St. Mary of the Angels had never seen anything like it before. The movement of people was phenomenal. The historical significance was extraordinary.

Five thousand friars! They all wanted to see Francis. They all wanted to listen to him, perhaps for the last time, maybe for the very first time. They all wanted, if they could, to spend a private moment with him, talking with him personally.

Five thousand friars! What a logistic headache! Such a large crowd brought about big problems. There were not enough food supplies. There was no capacity to maintain order and discipline. There were many on-the-spot predicaments which called for good sense and quick decision.

Five thousand friars! Where would they all stay? They went about hunting down branches and twigs from the surrounding area. They wove them into mats, and with the mats they constructed huts as far as the eye could see all around the Porziuncula chapel.

Five thousand friars! When Francis looked around and saw all the huts and watched the friars intent upon talking with God in prayer, he felt that everything was bubbling once again with the warmth and the sense of adventure of days gone by. So, not everything was lost. That this could happen with 5,000 was a sign that the spirit of the movement was still intact. And the friars themselves were really excited about their makeshift surroundings and the atmosphere of pilgrimage. They had nothing, and did not have to worry about anything. The old ideal was reemerging, and it was taking its revenge on conventional wisdom.

Five thousand friars! They all came in touch with the whole picture and became enthralled with it. Finally here was an encampment where God reigned supreme and where the only concern was how to put the Gospel into practice.

Five thousand friars! The news spread throughout the valley and up the hills and into the nearby cities. Assisi, Bettona, Perugia, Spello, Foligno. It filled the castles of nobles and the homes of peasants. The people were astonished. "Let us go see what is going on," they said, "and find out what is happening at St. Mary of the Angels." And, like the shepherds on that night in Bethlehem, they came carrying knapsacks full of gifts – bread and wine, fruit and grain. With such reinforcements, they descended upon the encampment of friars. Divine Providence taught another valuable lesson to everyone present.

The eighteenth chapter of the Fioretti describes this gathering, using the style of epic poetry. The combination of prose and lyrical verse gives voice to the encounter between liberty and law and the coming together of that last moment of spontaneity within the Order and that moment of self-definition and self-knowledge given by a formal rule.

During this chapter Brother Elias was elected vicar. He would be the man around whom developed the majority of arguments and contradictions regarding the Franciscan world. Either you were for him or against him; he was that kind a fellow that formed definite opinions in people.

For certain he both loved Francis and admired him intensely. And Francis returned the love, regardless of whatever particular currents of thought and certain style of living might have handed down over the years. But the love and admiration did not always translate into understanding and agreement. If there were a man who really did not comprehend the most characteristic features of Francis, it was probably Brother Elias. Yet there was a good deal of mutual esteem between them, even though so many critical remarks were thrown up into Elias' face. Francis, for sure, found in him something that he himself did not have, yet something he prized very highly. And Elias, for his part, continued to stand in awe over Francis' profound richness, which he could only perceive vaguely but which he felt needed to be protected and felt responsible for protecting. He did this in his own way, just as he would try to protect the life-like quality of a dream with the sword of battle. The spiritual goals of these two men, in fact, were worlds apart.

In contrast to Francis' emaciated physical appearance, Elias had a powerful voice and a commanding presence, which gave the impression that he was like a large oak tree providing shelter for Francis. When Francis spoke, Elias acted as his loudspeaker; he transmitted the message of that feeble voice which arose out of the depths of being which everybody held in such high esteem. And this esteem reflected a little bit of the spotlight upon the face of Elias, so that the friars might start respecting him too (so he hoped), since he was now the vicar of the one who founded the whole movement.

Jordan of Giano recounts in his Chronicles (17), which are very delightful stories to read, that Francis would sit at Brother Elias' feet during the meetings and, whenever he wanted to communicate something to that vast throng of friars, he would tug at the habit of his vicar. Elias would lean down to him, listen to what the saint had to say, and then standing up would bellow forth with a thunderous voice to make sure everyone could hear, even those farthest away, and would begin to shout: "Brothers, this is what Brother Francis is saying!..." In this way he would communicate the saint's desires and exhortations.

At this chapter there were not only friars; there were also prelates of the Church and people from all around. Some were devout, others were curious, some were spellbound, others were critical. Francis spoke to them, all, as much as he could. He talked about vice and virtue, urging them to be patient and to give witness. As was the custom of the time, he took the theme for the principal discourse from the Holy Scriptures. He began with Psalm 144 which says:

Blessed be the Lord, my rock,
who trains my arms for battle,
who prepares my hands for war.

During this massive gathering, Francis also presented a way of life which he had written down. We cannot say for sure whether this was the Earlier Rule (or Rule without Approbation) which is among the saint's writings or another similar document, but the preponderance of evidence points to the former. Historians do not agree if this was the year the Earlier Rule was presented or if it was held off for the general chapter of the following year. Whether it was the rule or a simple way of life, it became quite clear in 1221 that some sort of juridical norm or legal text was urgently needed. The great number of persons simply was not able to live together without a minimum of documentation. As limited as it was, it still would provide the necessary legislative content to bind everybody to God and to the community with a formal commitment. This document or rule, moreover, would eventually have to be approved by the pope.

Francis had already written more than one "rule" or "way of life." Their legal content was so poor that they were handled carelessly, were not taken seriously, and eventually got lost, because certain friars only considered important what they valued to be "real" juridical texts. The "great rules" of a Benedict or an Augustine appealed to many of the friars who joined the Order at someone else's suggestion or because it was the fashionable thing to do, without really understanding the spirit of Francis. Now they were very dissatisfied, and they thought they could upgrade their status by writing up documents with a whole line of rights and restrictions, without ever thinking whether or not they agreed with the spirit of Francis. He insisted, in fact, on referring to passages from the Gospels which endorsed a life filled with spontaneity, freedom, and Christian maturity. Francis was grossly misunderstood on this point, and this misinterpretation brought about a tangle of controversies down through the centuries over the Franciscan rule. This basic mistake has caused such awful rivalries in trying to understand the wrong thing with similar thought patterns that were in opposition to each other.

Thus the Chapter of Mats was a particularly important one because it tackled, to a certain degree, the question of giving a structure to the friars who belonged to the Order. This gathering produced a study in contrasts: on one side, the first-hand and deeply cherished memories of those primitive experiences of freedom and fervor were recounted with great emotion, while, at the same time, there was emerging the practical requirement for a set of rules.

Before letting the friars go back to where they came from, Francis made mention of the fact that the Order had not really been established in Germany, even though the friars had tried to settle there before. So, once more Francis tugged at Elias' habit and began to speak. Elias projected the saint's message:

"'Brothers, thus says the Brother [meaning Blessed Francis, who was called by the other brothers "The Brother" as it were par excellence]: there is a certain region called Germany, where there are devout Christian people, who, as you know, often pass through our country, perspiring under the heat of the sun, bearing large staves and wearing large boots, singing praises to God and the Saints, and visiting the shrines of the Saints. And because once the brothers who were sent to them were treated badly and returned, the Brother does not compel anyone to go to them; but to those who, inspired by zeal for God and for souls, may wish to go, he desires to give the same obedience that he gives to those who go beyond the sea, and even a broader one. If there are any who wish to go, let them rise and gather in a group aside.' And there were about ninety brothers inflamed with such a desire, offering themselves to death; and, gathering in a group aside, as they were commanded, they awaited the answer who, how

175

many, in what manner, and where they were to go" (*Jordan of Giano*, 17).

There was a friar who was terribly afraid of being martyred and he asked God constantly to save him from the heretics of Lombardy and from the cruelty of the Germans. Nonetheless, he was an enterprising sort of fellow. He was sure that the friars sent to Germany could possibly be martyred right away, he wanted to get to know them personally so that he could then have a head start on any future benefits. He had not succeeded in doing this with the Moroccan martyrs, so now he did not want to lose the chance with these presumed soon-to-be martyrs of Germany. Hence, he slipped into the group, acting as though he were part of it and asking each one of them who he was, where he came from, and so forth.

Among the ninety friars there was one from Mount Gargano of Puglia, Palmerius, who was a deacon. He was a consummate practical joker. When his turn came up to be interviewed, he grabbed that unlucky friar and held onto him by the hand, saying, "Now, you too are going to be one of us, and you are coming with us!" the more the friar insisted by saying that he did not want to go, the more tightly Palmerius held on to him and laughed until he constrained him by force. With this technique he made him miss the assignment of friars to the various other place. So, in the end, when everyone else had been told were they were going, Brother Elias found the ill-fated friar among the group of those who had volunteered to go to Germany. The desperate man protested: "I do not want to go to Germany!" He made such an issue of the whole thing that Elias, who did not have patience as one of his strong points, gave him a piece of his mind and told him to hurry up and decide what he was going to do. Now, the friar, apart from feeling afraid, was beginning to feel guilty. To decide upon his own destination meant that he was going back on his pledge to give himself completely to obedience.

"And thus, perplexed between the two choices and not finding any counsel within himself, he approached a brother who had been proved by many tribulations, namely, the brother who, as was said before, lost his breeches six times in Hungary, and asked advice of him" (*Jordan of Giano* 18). This friar advised him to do what any other friar would logically do: go to Brother Elias and submit to his decision. And Elias sent him to Germany. Now this brother is Brother Jordan of Giano who writes this down for you, who came to Germany under these circumstances, who escaped the fury of the Germans which he had dreaded, and who, together with Brother Caesar and the other brothers, first planted the Order of Minors in Germany" (*Jordan of Giano* 18).

At last the chapter was over. Francis gave permission to the friars to be on their way. They left St. Mary of the Porziuncula in the name of the Father and of the Son and of the Holy Spirit. Brother Caesar of Speyer was designated as the leader of the group departing for Germany, himself a well – educated German whom Francis used as his "expert consultant" for Sacred Scripture. As a fine "connoisseur" of people, Caesar picked the best of the bunch from the group of ninety friars. It is enough to give some of the names of the friars chosen in order to realize how good he was at choosing people. There was Brother John from Pian del Carpine (now called Magione), a village near Perugia, a noted preacher in Latin and in the Lombard dialect, who would be the first European to undertake a journey to the Far East (into the land of the Tartars) as the delegate and spokesman for Pope Innocent IV, there were Barnabas, also German, who could preach in both German and the Lombard dialect, and Thomas of Celano, the first and most well – known biographer of Saint Francis. Moreover, we find Joseph of Treviso, Abraham from Hungary, and Simon from Tuscany (who was the son of the countess of Collazzone near the town of Todi and a friend of

Emperor Otto IV's family). Also on the list were a German cleric named Conrad; three priests named Peter of Camerino, James, and Walter; Palmerius, that deacon with the sense of humor; and Jordan of Giano, also a deacon and the delightful story-teller of this whole adventure. There were also another German named Benedict von Soet and a Swabian named Henry. The names of the other are not written down any-where. All together there were twelve cleric friars and thirteen lay friars.

Before they all left for Germany from Italy, the group had to wait for Caesar of Speyer who was supposed to be finish-ing up some work which probably Francis gave him to do. They stayed around for three months in different parts of Lombardy while Caesar was in the Spoleto Valley. When they finally got under way, they passed through the following places: Trent, Bolzano, Bressanone, Vipiteno, Mittenwald (?), Matrey, and Augsburg, following the ancient Roman road. At Augsburg they received a warm and hearty welcome from the bishop and there, for the feast of St. Gall which fell on Octo-ber 13th (still in the year 1221), the friars of Germany held their first chapter. On that occasion Caesar commissioned the friars to set off for the various cities and territories.

The exuberance of the chapter was now followed by the peace and quiet at St. Mary of the Angels. Francis still lin-gered around the huts left empty by his friars. He thought about them tenderly while they traversed the dust-filled roads of the then-known world. Little by little the forest once again got the upper hand over the singing and the milling around of the thousands of friars. The birds returned as the uncontested landlords of the branches and the masters of the songs.

The friars were all gone, having set off as usual in the di-rection of the four winds to sign the world with the sign of the cross. The mood they left behind was that of adventure, risk, enthusiasm. Francis was still swept up by it. But now he felt as though he were bound by a chain. He realized that he was no longer able to go away; he could not act impulsively as he did when he went to Egypt. He was well aware of the price he had to pay for his absence in terms of the collapse of his ideals. He felt obliged to give good example; he had to keep an eye out so that no abuse would creep in, even though he was no longer the juridical leader. He might not have had any legal responsibilities, but he completely held on to that charismatic authority of the one who founded the Order, who got thousands of people involved in it, and who turned upside down the rural and urban societies, whether they were peaceful or turbulent. Nonetheless, Francis could not hold himself back from going on a preaching trip. He did not go too far so that he could keep in touch with what was happening at the Porziuncula. So he only went as far as Bologna because he knew he could be back in just a few days.

He set off. The people ran to see him. They were anxious to hear him, to touch him. He was considered a saint. The somewhat superstitious piety of the ordinary folk mingled with the curious attention he got from the educated people and from the clergy. People talked about him as though he were some legendary figure. And he knew he was admired. Along the way he preached and bore witness to the Gospel. He urged the people to be at peace with the prelates and the priests of the Holy Roman Church.

He arrived at Imola, not far from Bologna. He wanted to preach to the people, but, as was his custom, he first presented himself to the bishop to ask permission. The bishop, however, was very brusk with him.

"The bishop said to him: 'It is enough, Brother, that I preach to my people.' Bowing his head, St. Francis humbly went outside, and after a short time, he came back in. The bishop said to him: 'What do you want, Brother? What are you seeking now?' And the blessed Francis said: 'Lord, if a father drives his son out of one door, he must come back in by another.' Subdued by his humility, the bishop embraced him with a happy countenance and said: 'You and all your brothers may preach in my diocese in the future with my general permission, for your holy humility has merited this'" (2 *Cel.* 147).

He arrived in Bologna. This is where he had reproached his friars for building a stone house. Thomas of Spalato, who during this time was pursuing his studies at Bologna, related the theme of Francis' preaching: "Angels, human beings, and evil spirits" – a topic which everyone took seriously. On this particular occasion, the saint "spoke with such clarity and conviction about these three types of rational creatures that many learned people who were listening came away full of admiration for this unlettered man who spoke to them. He did not have the usual style of a preacher, but rather talked in a conversational tone. Actually, the content of his words was aimed at squelching their animosity toward each other and laying the foundation for new peace treaties. He wore a humble habit. His physical appearance did not account for much. His face was not very handsome. Yet, God conferred such efficacy upon his words that many noble families, who were so ferociously angry with each other because of enmities of days long past that they were causing a great amount of bloodshed, submitted to his advice for making peace" (*Hist. Sal. Spal.*).

A crowd of people gathered around him. They wanted to see him close up and touch him. The archbishop of Pisa, Frederick Visconti, who was present at that time in Bologna, recounted this event in a sermon he preached in 1265.

Francis felt a mixture of love and fear for Bologna. I do not have any documents to prove this, but this is my gut reaction. The learned people and, in fact, this whole city of higher education cast upon him an unusual spell; he was enchanted by its culture, which he both admired and was afraid of. And this only makes sense from the perspective of psychology. One thing is for sure: Francis was not unaffected by culture. Just the opposite! So many who want to make him appear as though he were the enemy of culture completely ignore – or pretend to ignore – that special appeal which attracts people of little formal education who become fascinated with the world of learning.

From Bologna Francis went around preaching, always keeping his eye fixed on the Porziuncula and traveling like a drawing compass which imbeds its point into the center and moves the pencil around the circumference. When he arrived at Terni, he started preaching in the town center, as he was in the habit of doing. The bishop, who was either nearby at his residence or in the plaza itself, listened attentively to this little brother from Assisi. As the sermon finished, however, he wanted to add something. He was a spiritual person and spoke from the perspective of a person who had an authentic spiritual grounding. Perhaps it was his intention to conclude Francis' exhortation, which focused on everybody's duty to praise and thank and worship God, with a practical and existential application.

So the bishop went on to say: "From the beginning, when our Lord planted and founded His Church, He had always enlightened it through holy people who have fostered it by word and example. But now in these latter days He has enlightened it through this poor, undistinguished and unlearned man named Francis. Therefore love and honor our Lord, and beware of sin; for He has not dealt so with any other nation."

Francis understood the allusion the bishop was making, and he figured out what the bishop's intentions really were. So, when the prelate had finished, he followed him into the cathedral, caught up to him, and knelt down before him, saying:

"My Lord Bishop, I assure you that no man in this world has ever done me such honor as you have done me this day. For other men say, 'This is a holy man', and attribute glory and holiness to me, rather than the Creator. But you are a discerning man and have distinguished between the precious and the worthless" (*Spec. Perf.* 45).

But not all the bishops were like this one from Terni nor were a carbon copy of Cardinal Hugoline. Francis had to win their friendship and admiration if he wanted to get permission to preach in their dioceses. And he never would have gone against the recommendation of the local bishop. In his Testament he was emphatic about saying that he still wanted to respect the permission of poor priests in the individual church where they dwelt, even if he were to have the wisdom of Solomon. These things were very important to him, and he knew how to accept the limitations which the institutional Church imposed, in view of the positive effect which the lessons they taught were able to bring about, in other words, for those who had reached a certain level of human maturity and are not plagued by childish attitudes and behavior.

Francis had the same kind of respect for all priests. The story goes that once he met up with a heretical leader who had an argument with a local parish priest because he was living with a woman. The heretic demanded: "Tell me, do we have to believe the words and trust as credible the behavior of somebody living in concubinage, somebody who dirties his hands by relating to a prostitute?" Francis said to him, in the presence of the priest: "I do not know if his hands are as dirty as that fellow described them; but I do believe with all my heart that, even if they were so, it would not at all lessen the strength and the efficacy of the holy sacraments. And it is by means of these very hands that God passes on his benefits and gifts to his people. Therefore, I kiss those hands, out of reverence for the sacraments which they administer and for the holiness of Him who has conferred upon them such power" (*An. Hist.*).

The preaching certainly enriched Francis' experience. He was no longer known as just a person who proclaimed a new kind of message. He was recognized as the saint from Assisi. He felt deeply the responsibilities which this role demanded of him, and, if ever he would use his reputation of holiness to bring souls to God, he was always afraid that he could be preaching about himself rather than about Jesus Christ whose servant he was. He preached to the people and instructed the friars. He spoke of conversion and praise, poverty and obedience, simplicity and love of God. These became the topics of his sermons.

"Once when blessed Francis was visiting the Lord Bishop of Ostia, who later became Pope Gregory (IX), he went out unobserved at dinnertime in order to ask alms from door to door. And when he returned, the Lord of Ostia had already gone in to table with many knights and nobles. But when the holy Father entered, he laid the alms that he had collected on the table before the Cardinal, and sat down beside him, for the Cardinal always wished that blessed Francis should sit next to him at table. The Cardinal was somewhat embarrassed to find that blessed Francis had gone out for alms and laid them on the table; but he said nothing at the time because of his guests.

"When blessed Francis had eaten a little, he took up his alms and in the name of the Lord God distributed a little to each of the knights and chaplains of the Lord Cardinal. And they all accepted them with great reverence and devotion, reaching out their hoods and sleeves; and some ate the alms, while others kept them out of devotion to him. After dinner the Cardinal entered his own apartment, taking blessed Francis with him. And stretching out his arms, he embraced him with great joy and gladness, saying, 'My simple brother, why have you shamed me today by going out for alms when you visit my house, which is a home for your friars?'"

Francis then explained how he could feel so much more satisfaction when he had a poor table rather than a rich one because a poor table was actually the table of the Lord. The cardinal, faced with the happy realization that this man really knew what true values actually were, he could say nothing more than this: "My son, do whatever seems good to you, for God is with you, and you with Him!" (*Spec. Perf.* 23).

We would have to say the very same thing.

THE SUFFERING OF FRANCIS

F rancis had thought that his dream would come true and that the Gospel would become the daily way of life for everybody. He believed that people in great numbers would leave power and abuse behind in order to embrace generosity and altruism. He had figured that the passages of the Gospel would be able to settle into people's hearts and replace the urge toward oppression, the thirst for worldly riches, the dream of earthly conquest, the drive toward greed, hatred, and contentions.

He was almost at the point of envisioning all these things already happening, or, perhaps better, he was always trying to see everything in the process of development within people, like yeast within dough. "Do not be afraid, little flock. ... The reign of God is like a woman who put some yeast into three bushels of flour. ... The reign of God is like a mustard seed." This is what the Gospel says; this is what Francis believed was happening. He thought that the yeast was having a leavening effect right before his very eyes, that the mustard seed was growing and was already a hearty little tree.

This illusion, however, took its toll on Francis physically. His eyes became more and more sunken from so much crying. His back became more and more stooped from carrying the burden. He had looked forward to an explosion of a gospel-based Christianity which would transform towns and territories. On the contrary, this leaven – splendid in quality and ripe for fermentation – did enter many a soul, but not much had penetrated deeply enough to bring about the difference he had hoped for.

He looked around. The crusade was moving ahead with its expressions of violence. People in business were fixed on running after material riches. Among the friars there were those who were just trying to make ends meet, others were not even doing that well. There were those who were too shrewd in the ways of the world or too dense in the ways of the Spirit to embark upon an ideal like this without first taking into consideration their personal convenience or, at least, their concern for their own well-being.

Francis was resigned to the disillusionment which the world situation caused him. He considered it necessary for the maturation process to happen. He understood that the human journey was tiresome, slow, and sometimes unsteady. This is why he was always able to smile at the people of the world as they made their way toward God. He gave them the benefit of the doubt and made excuses for their human weakness.

But the friars were another story!

The friars! They bound themselves with a cord just as he did. They went barefoot just as he did.

The friars! For him they were supposed to be that leaven or that mustard seed to bring about that worldwide conversion that he dreamed about and worked so hard to accomplish. Was it possible that even among the friars there would be people of little or no good will? One day, overcome with discouragement, he was to say:

"I love the brothers as much as I can; but if they would follow my footsteps, I would certainly love them even more and I would not make myself a stranger to them. For there are some among the number of superiors who draw them to other things, proposing to them the example of the ancients, and putting little value upon my admonitions. But what they are doing will be seen in the end,' and a little afterwards, when he was afflicted with grave infirmity, he raised himself upon his couch and said in vehemence of spirit: 'Who are these who have snatched my Order and that of my brothers out of my hands? If I go to the general chapter, I will show them what my will is'" (2 *Cel*. 188).

It was as though they had cut open his own flesh, had taken away part of himself.

To understand Francis also means to understand his pain. It was a pain, a suffering, that damaged even his soul. It was not the sorrow of a person who was forgotten or rejected because in reality, or at least in the minds of people, this was not the case, considering how much the friars revered him as their "living relic." He suffered because he was coming to see that the Gospel of Christ, to which he had committed his whole existence, was not even being understood. All of this weighed heavily upon his soul and his body, and it even had an influence upon the direction of his spiritual journey.

He was turning to a more ascetic and contemplative style of life in contrast to an active daily life, something like a parable path which people of good will take when they have given up on putting confidence in their own efforts to change the world. Francis retired to a more ethereal existence, leaving it only when he had to earn his daily bread.

Hence, poverty, which could have been an uplifting way of living, became a virtue to be practiced. Obedience, which could have been understood as standing ready to accept and cheerfully to be at the disposal of God's will as it appeared in daily life, became the mortification of someone who subjects oneself to endure other people's will in the name of God. Simplicity, which meant accepting the responsibility of guiding the friars, now was transformed into the risk of showing off and the temptation of seeking power.

Francis was aware of a shift in his own spiritual life and in the spirituality he was offering to others, and he had the good sense to admit this fact as a nonnegotiable part of his real-life situation. With pain, but also with much insight, he took up the task of reformulating his dreams and his ideals because he knew well the lesson which the situations and the events of life were teaching him.

Some time before, he had emphatically underscored the fundamental difference between his own inspiration and that of Benedict and Augustine. Now it seems that they were not so many worlds apart. For himself he would stay with his own lofty dreams through his contemplative prayer. For his friars, however, he would provide instruction on how to achieve the heights of holiness according to the grand masters, while touching upon his own particular point of view and his own experiences.

Like a vinedresser, he was "pruning" back his goals so that they would grow more vigorously. This is in the spirit of the Gospel! The Lord Jesus had spoken about the Father as the vinedresser who prunes his own vines so that they produce more fruit. Francis was cutting back for the same reason. He knew what it meant to relinquish, to prune. It is true that, if you pay close attention to the vine after a bunch of grapes has been cut off, you can find something like a teardrop covering the cut? Likewise, Francis shed his tears – both in secret and out in the open. And, because of these long and repeated bouts of sorrow, his health got worse.

It was necessary to prune. In order to do so, Francis retired to Fontecolombo (not far from Rieti) in early 1223. He went there with Brother Leo and Brother Bonizio of Bologna. He had to find the inspiration and the dedication to write the rule one more time. This rule was going to be a short one in which the church law would be presented clearly and precisely because the Holy See, which knew human tendencies all too well, was willing to approve a rule only if it was exact and explicit in those things pertaining to the expectations for human behavior.

Divine inspiration, distinctive and definitive as it is, is always accompanied by the influence of the human situation. We know that this human influence includes the framework of the circumstances and conditions within which we have to look for the will of God. For sure, it is not always simple to realize that point when other people are a help or a hindrance. In fact, in the great symphony of human experience, this is the most difficult note to play.

This was the actual situation Francis found himself in there at Fontecolombo nestled in the woods. He searched for the best solution by means of his dialogue with God, with Brothers Leo and Bonizio, with his fellow friars not physically near by but present in spirit, with the trees, and with the prompting of his own inner spirit. Like the nakedness of the winter season, he stripped the text he was obliged to prepare of any non-essential elements. Just as he knew that in the trees, the sap had to rise up strongly and quickly through the trunk and the branches in order to produce the buds and then the leaves and then the fruit with its seed, so too his inner being became filled with such power of prayer and meditation that the first signs of new life began to appear on the parchment:

"The rule and life of the Friars Minor is this: to observe the holy Gospel of our Lord Jesus Christ by living in obedience, without anything of their own, and in chastity. Brother Francis promises obedience and reverence to the Lord Pope Honorius and his canonically elected successors and to the Roman Church. And let the other brothers be bound to obey Brother Francis and his successors" (1223 *Rule*, 1-2).

The expressions he used were exact and precise. He repeated the terminology that had become hallowed by time. If we read the corresponding passage in the preceding rule (which today is called the "Earlier Rule" or the "Regula non Bullata" [that is, "Rule without Approbation"] or the 1221 Rule and, unfortunately, is the only existing text of all the rules before 1223), we find more or less the same ideas, but with less legal precision while the text visualizes the objective in a much more expansive context:

"In the name of the Father and of the Son and of the Holy Spirit. This is the life of the Gospel of Jesus Christ which Brother Francis asked the Lord Pope to be granted and confirmed for him; and he granted and confirmed it for him and his brothers present and to come. Brother Francis and whoever will be the head of this Order promises obedience and reverence to the Lord Pope Innocent and to his successors. And all the other brothers are bound to obey Brother Francis and his successors.

CHAPTER I:
The brothers must live without anything of their own and in chastity and in obedience
The rule and life of these brothers is this: to live in obedience, in chastity, and without anything of their own, and to follow the teaching and footprints of our Lord Jesus Christ, Who says: 'If you wish to be perfect, go' and 'sell' everything 'you have and give it to the poor, and you will have treasure in heaven; and come, follow me.' And, 'If anyone wishes to come after me, let him deny himself and take up his cross and follow me.' Again: 'If anyone wishes to come to me and does not hate father and mother and wife and children and brothers and sisters, and even his own life, he cannot be my disciple.' And: 'Everyone who has left father or mother, brothers or sisters, wife or children, houses or land because of me, 'shall receive a hundredfold and shall possess eternal life'" (1221 *Rule, Prologue* 1-4, 1:1-5).

In this comparison I would like to briefly take note of two very important points which have gotten lost in the rewrite:

the first one is how Francis understood the role of the pope (which, from a theological point of view, is so good that better theologians themselves would be well advised to study it).

The pope is seen as the one who has the charism to discern whether an interpretation of the Gospel is valid or not; this is his principal function ("... Francis asked the Lord Pope to be granted and confirmed for him; and he granted and confirmed it...")

The other important point that got lost in the confirmed Later Rule is how Francis specifies what it actually means to decide to observe the Gospel. It is not the Gospel understood in some generic sense to which someone would give a generic commitment, but "to follow the teaching and the footsteps of our Lord Jesus Christ, Who says..." (and then he cites some carefully selected texts). The Gospel, in fact, is open for all people to read; and, as a source of inspiration, it has an answer to any possible question which people or the times have generated because of their experiences or their abilities. The Gospel is beyond the realm of time, and every human person can give it flesh and put it into practice in life. Hence, when Francis cited those gospel passages with a similar theme as a way to shape his inspiration, he was choosing a particular course and direction to his spiritual journey.

The Gospel which Francis was proposing when he selected those citations put into the Earlier Rule was a Gospel very much influenced by his own particular experience. It was the experience of a person who had decided to give himself to God because he trusted completely in God's Word, who had set off in a certain direction while burning the bridges behind him. When we read the quotes from the Gospel in the Earlier Rule which we just mentioned, we see that they are precise and very enlightening. They are both points of departure and a context in which to live.

It was these particular treasures that Francis now decided to sacrifice, whether he had to or felt it was more opportune to do so. These were not the only limitations he made, even if we take into consideration just the first chapter. I have hardly touched on these two examples, but I hope they help us to imagine at least how much "sap" was contained in that stately but leafless "tree" which stood there at Fontecolombo in winter waiting for spring to arrive.

The date was June 11, 1223. The place was the Porziuncula. The event was the chapter, the Pentecost Chapter. The friars approved the rule which Francis had put together in a few chapters (twelve) – a rule which, most certainly, was already revised, checked over, and probably modified here and there by a body of experts, particularly Cardinal Hugoline.

This ongoing presence of Cardinal Hugoline, was reassuring. I say this because Hugoline had the well-being of Francis and his friars at heart. Without a doubt he was a prudent person, but he was also somebody who did not have his own personal interests in mind nor was he filled with envy and jealousy. What he wanted was the good of all – certainly that which he considered would be in the best interest of everybody. But how can I cast doubts about his integrity and credibility after more than seven hundred years when I know that Francis had such confidence in him?

When the Pentecost Chapter was over, the rule which the friars approved was examined carefully by the Roman Curia in an official manner without the counsel or suggestions of anyone endorsing Francis' position. Only after studying the whole text did Pope Honorius III, with the fullness of his papal authority approve the Rule of the Friars Minor with a pontifical decree entitled "Solet Annuere" (or in English "Accustomed to Accede"; these are the first words of the official text in Latin). This happened on November 29, 1223.

In order to remind the Friars Minor of their own modest origins, it is good to underline the fact that, while the papal decree approving the rule was the foundation of one of the most brilliant and singular experiences witnessed in the Church down through the ages, it was, at the same time, a very ordinary administrative document, repetitive and full of curial jargon, just like so many other legal decrees: "The Apostolic See is accustomed to accede to the pious requests and to be favorably disposed to grant the praiseworthy desire of its petitioners...".

A more personalized decree would not have made any difference to the curial officials and quite likely would have pleased the friars very much. But it is appropriate that the "Minors" remain minor (that is, no more important or prestigious than anyone else). Pope Honorius was the right person to make them understand that very thing. He was no Innocent III who came before him, nor was he a Gregory IX who succeeded him on the papal throne. Innocent and Gregory were popes who set their sights on making their dreams come true, on reaching their goals ahead, not just one, but many of them. For this reason they were highly enthusiastic and energetic. On the contrary, Honorius was a man of the moment; his concern was today. His agenda was to do what was possible right now, without surprise, without haste. It was a wonderful thing, and at the same time quite strange, in the Church that this particular man, rooted in the mundane and unimaginative present would be the one called to give his approval to one of the most adventurous experiments in the history of religious orders. Though his feet were on the ground, he knew how to value and appreciate the soaring of an eagle. This, perhaps, is the best way to pay tribute to Honorius.

Meanwhile, Brother Elias was still the head of the Order.

193

He was an organizer. He could give commands. He knew that he could incur both hate and love in people. Francis submitted to him as a good, exemplary religious; but he did not renounce the liveliness of that charism which still characterizes the Order and must give it so much richness.

Around Francis there were gathered, in a spiritual sense, those many people who felt a close bonding with him and who did not want to be identified with the enormous growth of the Order. Still, however, his presence was the source of some unrest, because he tried to balance the two different basic concepts which we have already talked about. To put this restlessness into perspective, we have to realize that this particular instability or struggle was nothing more than new life bursting forth.

It is typical of the Franciscan world that any attempt to institutionalize will sooner or later go through the cycle of renovation but is never destroyed in the process. This is what is meant by experiencing daily the power of the leaven in living the Gospel.

THE PRAYER OF ST. FRANCIS

Francis was no longer the minister general, but he still remained the charismatic leader of the Order. He was becoming melancholy and downcast because he felt that the others neither understood him nor really followed after him. Everybody loved him, it is true. And there was no friar who did not admire him, but... this "but" had to do with the everyday practical life-style which he envisioned as that incentive which comes from love to bring to completion what he had perceived within himself. Instead, many of the friars considered this path too difficult and exhausting, and, every once in a while, they introduced some sort of means to detract from it or run away from it. In this way the actual style of living the Gospel that Francis himself was living was being ignored.

After he had handed over the concerns of being the head of the Order first to Brother Peter Catanii and then to Brother Elias, Francis felt the desire to be alone with God swelling up inside of him again. He had already gone off to a solitary place in order to put together the rule which was subsequently approved by Rome. Solitude was a comfort to him, and it gave him a standard by which he could measure what it meant to live in God's presence and to stand before the rest of creation. But his vocation was not to be a hermit. If that peace and quiet of prayer invigorated him, this solitude and this energy were not just ends in themselves. Rather, every time God graced him with some gift, he knew that he always had to share it with other people.

As Christmas of 1223 was approaching, Francis went to Sir John Velita, a gentleman from Greccio, a little town perched on the ridge of a mountain overlooking the Rieti Valley. It was likely that Francis had retired to that area to fast and pray during the season of Advent, or maybe he was just passing through during one of his journeys between Assisi and Rome. John Velita had given the friars a rocky place on the mountainside not far from the city; it was his gift to them. He owned the property which was filled with trees and large boulders ideal for solitude; it was well suited for meditation and retreat. The saint went to Sir John with this proposal:

"If you want us to celebrate the present feast of our Lord at Greccio, go with haste and diligently prepare what I tell you. For I wish to do something that will recall to memory the little Child who was born in Bethlehem and set before our bodily eyes in some way the inconveniences of his infant needs, how he lay in a manger, how, with an ox and an ass standing by, he lay upon the hay where he had been placed" (1 *Cel.* 84).

John Velita was so happy to do this, and he set himself to the task of making sure everything was organized. We do not know exactly what he had to organize and prepare, but it must have been a few simple things, like informing the farmers and peasants of the surrounding area passing the word onto the artisans of Greccio, and getting the news to some of the people from the nearby villages. The new idea launched by Francis created quite a bit of enthusiasm among those people who were ordinarily accustomed to waiting in the darkness of the longest nights of winter for the coming of dawn so that they could begin working without wasting any oil in their lamps.

So, on this night before Christmas, the people of Greccio deserted the parish and country churches and went to celebrate the Nativity at the place chosen by Francis. Whole families arrived, carrying an oil lamp or a torch or a few twigs ignited to illuminate their path and to create a festive atmosphere. It was such an intimate and simple event; our own imagination can embellish the picture with color and music from the bagpipes. It was so good for the people to come together and to prepare the manger by filling it with hay and straw and bringing in a donkey and a cow taken from Sir John's barn. The actual scene was built upon a tradition passed on long ago down through the centuries because the Gospel, in fact, makes no mention of an ass or an ox.

Francis was overcome with joy. Finally, with a bit of imagination, he was able to realize the dream of actually seeing and hearing and touching the real moment when his Lord Jesus Christ was born. Just as he "touched" God when he received the Eucharist (see the first of Francis' "Admonitions"), so the manger and the cow and the donkey made Jesus' birth in poverty alive and present. And Jesus came down among the people during the celebration of the Mass. It was a solemn Mass. Francis, since he was not a priest, wanted to exercise his proper function as a deacon; so he chanted the Gospel which narrated the birth of Jesus Christ; following that came the homily. From here we turn to Thomas of Celano to continue the story:
"And his voice was a strong voice, a sweet voice, a clear voice, a sonorous voice, inviting all to the highest rewards. Then he preached to the people standing about, and he spoke charming words concerning the nativity of the poor King and the little town of Bethlehem. Frequently too, when he wished to call Christ 'Jesus,' he would call him simply the 'Child of Bethlehem,' aglow with overflowing love for him; and speaking the word 'Bethlehem,' his voice was more like the bleating

of a sheep. His mouth was filled more with sweet affection than with words. Besides, when he spoke the name 'Child of Bethlehem' or 'Jesus,' his tongue licked his lips, as it were, relishing and savoring with pleased palate the sweetness of the words" (1 *Cel*. 86).

That Christmas in Greccio was a memorable one and was the beginning of our traditional manger scene today. In some places, like Italy, there are papier-mache grottoes filled with lights and little plaster statues heading toward the holy grotto to take their gifts along some unlikely path covered with flour to replicate snow. For some of us this is no more than family tradition or folklore, but for Francis this was prayer and contemplation. This is how he prayed: he became absorbed in prayer in such a way that he could create situations that would transform prayer into real life and real life into prayer.

December of 1223 was over. The spring of 1224 came to revive the hopes of those who were content and placated that the rule received papal approval and who were thinking about the future of the Order which was already well established within the Catholic Church. At the end of that spring was the Pentecost Chapter which, in the year 1224, fell on June second. This was the first general chapter in which they did not have to talk about the rule; their only topic for discussion was implementing spiritually and corporately what had already been approved definitively and which consequently became a way to fulfill the demands of church law. It was also natural to consider expanding the Order beyond its present geographical borders; for example, it was not yet in England. The chapter easily took care of this need with clarity of vision. Brother Elias knew how to organize and, above all, knew what he wanted.

To chronicle the arrival of the friars in England, we have a text by Thomas of Eccleston written certainly after 1250 and most likely around 1258. It had fifteen chapters or stones. Thomas of Eccleston literally recorded how the first friars in England used to discuss spiritual topics in the evening, sitting around a fire and sipping a glass of beer. He recounted their arrival and the Franciscans' first experience in that country. His treatise helps us to understand the mood of the Order at that time when it was expanding all over the place and was feeling quite sure of itself. The adventure in England certainly was not full of the fear and the doubt that characterized the advance into Germany. The friars were confronted, however, with some simple difficulties, but they knew that they had the powerful organization of the Order to back them up. Herein lies the essential difference between Thomas of Eccleston and Jordan of Giano who had listed the likelihood of martyrdom among the possible ways to resolve the situation.

Nine friars were sent to England; Brother Agnellus of Pisa was their leader.

"These nine friars were charitably transported to England and courteously provided for by the monks of Fecamp. When they had come to Canterbury, they remained for two days at the priory of the Holy Trinity. Immediately four of them went to London, namely, Brother Richard of Ingworth, Brother Richard of Devon, Brother Henry and Brother Meltoratus. The other five, however, went to the priests' hospital where they remained until they could provide a place for themselves. Shortly thereafter a small room was given to them within a school house where they remained almost continuously shut in day after day. But, when the students had returned home in the evening, they went into the schoolhouse where they sat and built a fire for themselves; and they sat next to it and sometimes, when they had to have their collation, they put on the fire a little pot containing the dregs of beer, and they dipped a cup into the pot and each drank in turn and spoke some words of edification" (*Eccleston* 1).

It was all so typically British, you see.

The friars started off in France and landed in England on September 10, 1224.

Francis had never been a healthy and robust man. Nonetheless, he pushed his strength to the limit to do what was possible and sometimes what was impossible. But now he was quite ill. His physical make-up could no longer hide sickness of body nor his suffering of soul. Everything that had happened, even those things that came about with his approval and participation, disheartened him so much, as we have seen, and caused him to turn to God as his refuge. He was not, however, running away, as we have mentioned before. He was a Christian who accepted and understood history; he was capable enough of carrying (not just enduring) the sorrows and disappointments of life.

The fact that Francis was devoting more and more time to prayer, which was increasingly taking on a more mystical character, puts us in touch with the plan of God to continue that same revolution which he first entrusted to Francis as a radical renewal of gospel living; now, however, it was taking on a somewhat different perspective – a more intimate contact with God. To achieve this purpose, Francis became more and more a person of prayer while still maintaining a balance in his commitment to give others good example.

Once he put behind him the so-called active life, Francis, because of his ill health, could no longer travel through the city centers of Italy and visit the castles and cottages, as in the time of his youth. He was well aware, however, of the reputation he had among the people. So, even though he defined himself as a simple and unlettered person and so many people figured that he was against any kind of scholarship, he chose a new apostolic endeavor: the written word. He began to send out letters.

200

If, using today's standards, Francis were to be called a journalist, that would seem like a rather trite and worn-out analogy, but this is exactly what he was. He had that intuition to know the influence which a person with a high moral reputation would have on people if he would start writing for the sake of teaching and admonishing and involving other people in regard to one's own mission. And write he did. Or he dictated to Brother Leo so that he could capture on paper the summary of everything he was doing or put in a nutshell what his ideals really were.

He wrote a circular letter entitled "A Letter to the Rulers of the Peoples." He did not make any distinction between the good ones and the evil ones, between those who were friends and those who were enemies. With the same simplicity with which he spoke to God in prayer, he addressed the important people of the earth. He spoke to them without beating around the bush, without hurling any lightning bolts, without resorting to all those diplomatic niceties.

"Pause and reflect." This is how the letter to the world's leaders begins. What were all those mayors and legislators and military leaders supposed to stop and think about?

"Pause and reflect, for the day of death is approaching. I beg you, therefore, with all possible respect, not to forget the Lord or turn away from His commandments by reason of the cares and preoccupations of this world... Therefore, I firmly advise you, my lords, to put aside all care and preoccupations and receive with joy the most holy Body and the most holy Blood of our Lord Jesus Christ in holy remembrance of Him" (*LRul* 2-3, 6).

This topic of the Eucharist was Francis' "hobby-horse." As he stated in his Testament, "I see nothing corporal, of the Most High Son of God in this world except His Most holy Body and Blood" (10) consecrated in the Eucharist. He always felt the need to see and touch things because his earthly and spiritual life had to be real and concrete for him. It is important to understand this "need for the physical" on the part of Francis in order to have as clear and complete a notion of his spiritual experience as possible. This is why I soon intend to analyze the "body language" of our saint.

He exhorted the rulers of the people to honor God in public in the midst of their people. Moreover, he asked those who spread the news to remind the people every evening of their responsibility to give God praise and thanks. This demand was something new and was probably inspired by the Moslem muezzins who called people to prayer from the top of the minarets. Though he certainly wanted the Moslems to turn to Christ by means of the gift of faith rather than by the force of military conquest, he knew how to learn quite a few positive things from meeting them. A few experts have already written quite a bit about this topic, but perhaps much more needs to be written and promulgated in order to understand – and to let Francis instruct us about – that interreligious dialogue which gives life to the Church.

Francis also wrote to his friars and to the clergy in general. He composed both circular letters and personal letters. Those he could not reach by means of preaching or example, he reached by writing. And in these letters, once again, we find the Eucharist as the central theme. But he did not only talk about the Eucharist. To a certain minister of the friars (we do not know who it was or when he was addressed), Francis wrote about some very moving things:

"I wish you to know that if you love the Lord God and me, his servant and yours – if you have acted in this manner: that is, there should not be any brother in the world who has sinned, however much he may have possibly sinned, who after he has looked into your eyes, would go away without having received your mercy, if he is looking for mercy. And if he were not to seek mercy, you should ask him if he wants mercy. And if he should sin thereafter a thousand times before your very eyes, love him more than me so that you may draw him back to the Lord. Always be merciful to brothers such as these. And announce this to the guardians, as you can, that on your part you are resolved to act in this way" (*LMin* 9-12).

Furthermore, he wrote a letter to all the faithful which is pretty much a compendium of everything he preached and recommended. "Since I am the servant of all, I am obliged to serve all and to administer to them the fragrant words of my Lord" (1 *LF* 2).

In this letter he speaks about the Son of God who became a human being to fulfill the Father's will and to save us. Him, therefore, we all must love and praise as God by observing his will. To him we must confess our sins, and from him receive forgiveness. Because of him we must judge others with mercy and help those in need. For him we must get rid of our vices – especially hatred – and do as much good as we can, following his example as Christ the Lord. The benefit of such behavior on our part and of our faith will be, to praise God, which is the most wonderful thing a human being can do.

What happens if we do not do all this? As if to reply to this questions, Francis, at the end of his exhortation, describes in very realistic terms the death of someone who had made the choice of forgetting about God. When near death, that person will look for help from financial assets and from those things placed ahead of God, and, all alone, will become aware of that bitter isolation in which he or she is situated at the moment of death.

Then, in closing the letter, Francis writes: "In that love which is God, I Brother Francis, the least of your servants and worthy only to kiss your feet, beg and implore all those to whom this letter comes to hear these words of our Lord Jesus

Christ in a spirit of humility and love, putting them into practice with all gentleness and observing them perfectly. Those who cannot read should have them read to them often and keep them ever before their eyes, by persevering in doing good to the last, because they are 'spirit and life.' Those who fail to do this shall be held to account for it before the judgment-seat of Christ at the last day. And may God, Father, Son, and Holy Spirit, bless those who welcome them and grasp them and send copies to others, if they persevere in them to the last" (1 *LF* 86-89).

There is no need to explain how Francis, in his respect for the written word, was deeply affected by a mentality which for us seems so far away, that was due to the scarcity of writing materials and the minimal number of people who were able to read.

The Order was firmly in the hands of the holy Roman Church and in the hands of Brother Elias. Francis was told what he felt he was supposed to say to the friars and to the people. Now he felt the need to exit from the everyday world a bit more. He had plenty of things to talk over with God. He had to evaluate once again his experiences and his human disappointments. As usual, he was looking for a balance between his human experiences and his spiritual journey; this he could do only in solitary places where the person is quiet and God alone speaks. Having just come from an experience of pain, he felt attracted to Christ who, after the experience of Gethsemane and the betrayal of his disciples, mounted the wood of the cross.

It was August by then. The air was thick with crickets and cicada, stuffy with heat, and heavy with sudden thunderstorms. With Leo, Masseo, Tancredius, Sylvester, and Illuminatus, Francis left for the area of Tuscany.

There was a mountain in Tuscany with lots of trees and

very rocky, very inaccessible and quite high, with deep cool clefts in the rock and covered over with moss. Many years before Count Orlando of Chiusi donated it to him as a sign of devotion with the hope that it could be of some service in Francis' encounters with God. Now was the time for him to climb up the mountain named Verna whose peak was hidden when the clouds hung low. The man of God walked with some difficulty, as though he were pulled along by an inner voice that kept calling out to him. He knew that something out of the ordinary was beginning to take shape within him among these mountain boulders.

He trudged along. He went up higher. He scouted out the area. Finally he found a place that he liked. It was not the one which the count had excitedly gotten ready for him when he eagerly came there to pay his respects to the holy father who had arrived on his land. Francis chose another place, a sharp, overhanging precipice that would scare anybody. This place was so steep that his companions found it hard to throw down the trunk of a tree to form a bridge over the fissure between the accessible part of the mountain and what jutted out on the other side of the crevice.

Francis felt the need to be alone, not in order to avoid people, but in order to see and touch his God in an experience that he already knew from his premonition would be new and exceptional. He also chose a particular way of living: staying all by himself, taking a crust of bread or a sip of water only when Brother Leo figured it was the right time. Francis commanded: "That is the way of life which I place upon myself and on you" (*Fior. Stig.* 2).

Thomas of Celano recounted (1 *Cel.* 93) that more or less during this time (it is not important whether it was the first or a subsequent stay on La Verna) Francis once again wanted to come in contact with the "judgment of God." He had already done this at the beginning of his conversion experience, and now, since he felt that he was approaching a new and unusual happening, he needed to question God and to prepare himself to fulfill as totally as possible the will of his Father in heaven. So, he picked up the book of the Gospels, made the sign of the cross, and opened it. This time his eyes fell on that gospel passage which forewarned the disciples about the passion of the Lord. Once more he opened the book and did the same thing a third time; all of the citations from the Gospel spoke of the passion of the Lord. The forewarning was most clear. Francis shuttered, mind and soul, with joy and sorrow both together.

"May the power of your love, 0 Lord, fiery and sweet as honey, wean my heart from all that is under heaven, so that I may die for love of your love, you who were so good as to die for love of my love."

Thus Francis prayed in the depths of his spirit.

He began the Lent in honor of St. Michael the archangel in the middle of August (this was about forty days of prayer and fasting starting after the feast of the Assumption on August 15 in preparation for St. Michael's feastday on September 29). Brother Leo was the only person permitted to share some moments with the man of God, and he was most respectful of this responsibility.

"O Lord, open my lips!" he would shout out as he placed his foot on that tree trunk which acted as a bridge between the world of the friars and the solitude of the saint. Francis did not always respond, and so Brother Leo would not dare move any farther forward because he was ordered by Francis not to cross the bridge unless he got a specific invitation either during the day when he would bring a bit of bread and a cup of water or at night when he would pray Matins (Office of Readings) with him.

To tell the truth, Brother Leo recounted much later in his life that he disobeyed Francis from time to time only to make sure that Francis was okay. We can easily forgive this sort of disobedience! He also recalls that more than once (and always when he was not following Francis' orders) he witnessed a vision or a conversation between the saint and God. Human imagination and the reputation for holiness which surrounded Francis caused so many stories about his vision and his mystical dialogues to flourish; any eager reader can readily discover this among the various ancient works about the saint, especially "The Considerations on the Holy Stigmata" which many authors include as part of the Fioretti.

Just as Francis regarded so highly the events of Jesus' early life after he recreated the poverty of his birth in Bethlehem with his Christmas at Greccio, so now there welled up in him another desire:

"My Lord Jesus Christ, I pray You to grant me two graces before I die: the first is that during my life I may feel in my soul and in my body, as much as possible, that pain which You, dear Jesus, sustained in the hour of Your most bitter Passion. The second is that I may feel in my heart, as much as possible, that excessive love with which You, 0 Son of God, were inflamed in willingly enduring such suffering for us sinners" (*Fior. Stig. 3*).

His prayer was charged with emotion and fixed on the desire for union. By this time Francis felt that he had to take on the experience Christ's bitter sufferings himself in order to really reflect on it in his own heart or to talk with any credibility about it to other people. How could he speak with conviction and depth if he did not possess that reality which seared his soul and branded the experience onto his heart?

Francis was in ecstasy. With his eyes closed to the material world, he savored the passion of Christ, just as with a kiss a person tastes the flavor of love.

Right before those eyes which were now shut and which were having so much difficulty seeing, there began to appear, little by little, the form of a cross. It was far in the distance; the image was dim; it looked as though it was being supported by the wings of a seraph. There were six wings – two covering the head, two the body, two the feet. At the center of the cross was the figure of a crucified human being.

The reality he experienced was so wonderful and yet so painful. In it joy and suffering were fused together into a combination of feelings which we would call love. And as the vision slowly faded into the blue of the sky, there opened like a flower on his chest, on his right and left hands, and on his two feet five actual wounds which hurt terribly but which filled him with such joy. They were the color of fresh blood – bright red.

This most powerful experience by which he shared with Christ the pain of the cross, marked his body with the signs of the passion. It was similar to that situation when a person, exhausted from suffering, shows the tell-tale signs of the pain on a face that looks absolutely drained or on a body that is withered. It goes to prove that the soul touches the body, and the body, in turn, provides a physical dimension to the elation and the travails of the soul.

This event was something completely new; it had never before been historically substantiated. And it happened right there on the slopes of Mount La Verna in full view of that fissure in the rocks which opened to a great hole in the earth and which, according to popular legends, first broke open at the moment when Christ died on the cross and Golgotha trembled in terror.

This was the Stigmata of St. Francis. The five wounds appeared on his flesh. It was the incarnation of his very prayer.

It was a souvenir and an outward sign of that intense pain he suffered when he contemplated the crucifixion of the Son of God.

At that very moment, "All of Mount La Verna seemed to be on fire with very bright flames, which shone on the night and illumined the various surrounding mountains and valleys more clearly than if the sun were shining over the earth" (*Fior. Stig.* 3).

The date was September 14, 1224.

THE BEGINNING OF THE CANTICLE

F rancis spent a few more days on Mount LaVerna in order to become used to his new, overwhelming, and overpowering experience as the prevailing way he would now be living his life. This is always what he did at those critical turning-points of his life when he came face to face with an experience that was completely new. He invariably allowed himself a period of reclusion and prayer to usher a new level of maturity into his life.

So, he stayed there in prayer and contemplation. At the end of September, when he finally went down the mountain, the wounds made his feet and hands and side feel as though they were on fire. He could not hide them from his most intimate friends like Brother Leo; from the others, however, he tried to conceal the wounds by covering the palm of his hands with the sleeve of his habit and his feet with bandages. The wounds prevented him from walking, and his feverish condition, which was visible in his eyes, forced him to use a donkey to get about. He kept his eyes lowered because he felt ashamed that he had to break the Rule. The Rule, in fact, prohibited the friars from traveling on horseback, and Francis, though he was quite lenient in interpreting the needs of the friars, was not as tolerant of what was necessary for his own situation, just like so many people who feel very keenly their responsibility of leadership.

The little group made its way along the footpaths down the mountain like a procession. Francis sometimes was at the head of the line leading his companions, sometimes he brought up the rear following them. As they walked along, they prayed and they meditated. Once they reached the valley, they took the way that headed for Umbria. By then, when Francis traveled over the roads of Tuscany and Umbria, it were as though a saint was passing by, especially after the news had spread far and wide about the miraculous event which took place on La Verna.

Everyone was talking about the secret of the stigmata, but very few people – only those who were most reliable and trustworthy – managed to have any visible proof of its authenticity. Francis was most protective about guarding the secret, but he could not entirely prevent something from leaking out. The very fact that he became so preoccupied about keeping the wounds hidden, made people all the more interested in finding out what happened and in paying close attention to him. The bandages he wore and the difficulty he had walking spoke all too clearly about what was going on. To tell the truth, Francis himself would have talked about the wounds if he could be sure that the people would give praise and glory to God for so great an event. The people, however, and in particular the folks of the Middle Ages, were much too prone to get caught up in their unhealthy fascination with relics for him to be able to put any trust in them. So, under the circumstances, Francis was subjected to veneration, praise, and curiosity by the people wherever along the road they came upon the villages, towns, and country hamlets.

He passed through Borgo San Sepolcro in a way fit for a king: the people went to meet him, shouting, "Behold the saint! Behold the saint!" And they tried to touch him and grab him all over. Francis, however, was so completely absorbed with God in contemplative prayer – as the Fioretti tells the story – that he did not even realize that he had passed through that little town. They went from there and arrived that evening in a place called Montecasale where they stayed for a few days to rest up. Francis was nonetheless concerned about sending back the peasant who had accompanied him as a guide for the donkey so that he would not be away from his family for too long a time. Along with this peasant he also sent two of the friars who came with him back to their hermitage on Mount La Verna.

From Montecasale he reached Umbria; the destination was not too far away now. He did not get very far, however, because the inhabitants of Città di Castello set up a roadblock and held him captive for a good month simply because they wanted to have him with them. They said that, when he would pass by, many miracles would occur (these people, you know, relished miracles and believed in them immensely). Basically that mentality was not too much different than the one we find in our day.

When Francis arrived at St. Mary of the Angels, it was the dead of winter and probably it was really cold in the Spoleto Valley, which has the reputation, even today, of being so foggy and damp. In regard to this point, the Fioretti attests to a new astonishing event:

"When they were near [St. Mary of the Angels], Brother Leo looked up and gazed toward the holy place of St. Mary. As he looked, he saw a very beautiful cross, on which there was hanging the figure of Christ crucified, going before the face of St. Francis, who was riding ahead of him. And he clearly saw that the wonderful cross went before the face of St. Francis in such a way that when he stopped, it stopped, and when it went on, it likewise went on, and wherever St. Francis went, it preceded him. And that cross was so bright that not only did it shine in St. Francis' face, but it also illumined the air all around, and Brother Leo could see everything in a clear light. And it lasted until St. Francis entered the Place of St. Mary of the Angels" (*Fior. Stig.* 4).

At last Francis was back in the place he loved the most. He returned to give praise to our Lady in the chapel of the Porziuncula and to a small hut made of twigs a bit distant from the chapel. The wounds were so very painful; his sight was fading; his stomach could not take it any longer. This was the real physical situation behind the holiness of this man of God. Even though the veneration and the praise of the friars certainly made him feel better on the inside, it was not enough to take away his suffering. The illnesses, however, did not prevent Francis from praying nor did they take away the opportunities to deepen his spiritual life. How could he not praise the Lord? Reaching this stage of his life was like climbing a mountain and seeing that spectacular panorama and a horizon which grew broader and broader the higher he went. How could he help not glorifying his God, even though his hands were bloody and his energy level was at the point of complete collapse?

I believe that, if we really want to understand this particular time in Francis' life when so much joy blossomed forth from his pain, we have to liken Francis to a person scaling a rocky bluff tied to a cord secured by a nail and hanging dangerously over the abyss that opens up below; the rock-climber suffers the blizzards and the cold, the darkness of the night and the never-ending loneliness, moving ahead just foot by foot. The hands are aching, and the whole body is tense and in pain, while the heart is singing because the climber knows where he came from and where he is headed to conquer the mountaintop from which he will enjoy a most marvelous scene that only those whose spirit is severely confined would not manage to understand.

So, Francis would serenade each of his burdens, singing,

"Such is the good that I await and expect that each of my pains is for me a delight."

The key to the solution of all human suffering is in this approach. When, to find a reason for suffering, someone keeps asking, "Why? Why? Why me, if God is supposed to be so good?", then that person needs to remember the rock-climber and to recall the experience of Francis who grasped the meaning of the Gospel of his Lord Jesus Christ. If we honestly reflect on ourselves, in fact, we realize how right Francis was. When we ask "why?", there is a reason behind our question: we are having difficulty placing ourselves in the state of mind of that climber who knows his origins and his destination. In other words, we are not aiming toward the future; so the present weighs heavy upon us and seems to make little sense by itself. Here we see how, humanly speaking, Christianity is so magnificent that we have to rediscover it if we want to live life to the fullest.

The weather was still quite cold in the winter between 1224 and 1225 when Francis felt the need to communicate to the world everything that the Lord had made him understand during the last experiences he had. Neither the crucifixion of La Verna nor the popularity and the veneration of the people, as well as of the friars, weakened that vital rhythm which was characteristic of Francis' own life from the beginning and which he instilled in the souls of the first companions. Once again his life developed after the model of a beating heart: there were moments of rest and moments of impulse – times in solitude to meditate upon and mature one's experiences, and times to go forth throughout the world to proclaim how significant and meaningful his recent encounter with the Lord really was. Then, back to solitude; and again, out to preach.

The friars at the Porziuncula found a small donkey and perhaps a person from the countryside who could lead the beast. With great difficulty Francis mounted the donkey's back and set out to preach Christ crucified which is not just absurdity and pain, but also resurrection.

It was a short trip, owing to Francis' physical condition. He traveled around Umbria for a while; then he headed toward the Marches which would echo that first journey he made with Brother Giles when the young girls ran away from them after stealing a glimpse of them because they appeared so disheveled. This time, however, the girls did not dash away any more, and the people ran to see the saint, to touch him and, beyond any thought of getting a blessing, to rip off a piece of his habit to keep as a relic. Those who could, already started to secure his clothes for themselves, in exchange for a habit that was not so worn out (none was new because he would not have wanted that!) and recently laundered. Thus it was that the habits of Francis had the occasion to multiply.

When the trees began to put forth their green foliage and to gently quake in the breeze, Francis no longer could put up with the draining toll which the mission was taking on him. The Lord indicated to him that he must reshape and reduce his physical activity; so, he returned to his favorite valley. This time he did not stop at the Porziuncula. He was taken to San Damiano where by now there had developed a wonderful community of sisters who had followed St. Clare in living a new style of evangelical and penitential life.

He saw once again the image of Christ which motivated his early beginnings. He saw the little church which he had rebuilt with his own hands. With consummate humility he asked those women who saw themselves as his spiritual daughters to be so kind as to give him a hut alongside the monastery where he could pray and be taken care of by hands more gentle and tender than the gnarled ones of his companions.

The time that Francis spent at San Damiano were very

eventful days. For the nuns, he signified the living presence of a saint and the suffering presence of a brother who was in much pain and needed a little cleaning up, a bit more tender loving care, and some softer clothes to cover his wounds. He was almost blind and felt so dependent upon the kindness of others. As a real Christian, Francis did not accentuate his own misery, but rather emphasized the charity of those who were near at hand and were looking after him with such affection. He thanked God for all that had happened to him and for these sisters who were so like him in their compassion and their love.

The account given in the Legend of Perugia (n. 43) states that Francis spent a good fifty days or more at San Damiano. The events that we are going to relate happened in a span of time between April and May, 1225; this is the best season of the year to look out over the Spoleto Valley from San Damiano. Of this valley Francis used to say: "I have never seen anything more delightful than my Spoleto Valley." And he could not be wrong.

"Francis could not bear the light of the sun during the day or the light of the fire at night. He constantly remained in darkness inside the house in his cell. His eyes caused him so much pain that he could neither lie down or sleep, so to speak, which was very bad for his eyes and for his health. ... One night, as he was thinking of all the tribulations he was enduring, he felt sorry for himself and said interiorly: 'Lord, help me in my infirmities so that I may have the strength to bear them patiently!' And suddenly he heard a voice in spirit: 'Tell me, Brother, if, in compensation for your sufferings and tribulations you were given an immense and precious treasure: the whole mass of the earth changed into pure gold, pebbles into precious stones, and the water of the rivers into perfume, would you not regard the pebbles and the water as nothing compared to such a treasure? Would you not rejoice?'

217

Blessed Francis answered: 'Lord, it would be a very great, very precious, and inestimable treasure beyond all that one can love and desire!' 'Well, Brother,' the voice said, 'be glad and joyful in the midst of your infirmities and tribulations: as of now, live in peace as if you were already sharing my kingdom'" (*Leg. Perug.* 43).

In the morning he was so convinced that the conversation during the night with the Spirit was real that he called his companions together and told them the story: if the emperor would give to someone a kingdom or even his whole empire, would that person not have to be content? Then why should I not be satisfied with being called to possess the reign of God? Charged with great enthusiasm given him by this certainty, he set himself to the task of meditating and contemplating with immense joy the marvelous things which God – who is for us a Father – is doing.

He formulated a joyous song of praise and thanksgiving. With a singing voice somewhat tired but still in tune, he began to chant. The sweet Umbrian countryside listened to the Canticle of Brother Sun, the very first significant praise of God in that brand new language called Italian.

> *Most high, all-powerful, all good, Lord!*
>   *All praise is yours, all glory, all honor, and all blessing.*
> *To you alone, Most High, do they belong.*
>   *No mortal lips are worthy to pronounce your name.*
> *All praise be yours, my Lord, through all that you have made,*
>   *And first my lord Brother Sun,*
>   *Who brings the day; and light you give to us through him.*
> *How beautiful is he, how radiant in all his splendor!*
>   *Of you, Most High, he bears the likeness.*
> *All praise be yours, my Lord, through Sister Moon and Stars;*
>   *In the heavens you have made them, bright and precious and fair.*

All praise be yours, my Lord, through Brothers Wind and Air,
And fair and stormy, all the weather's moods,
By which you cherish all that you have made.
All praise be yours, my Lord, through Sister Water,
So useful, lowly, precious and pure.
All praise be yours, my Lord, through Brother Fire,
Through whom you brighten up the night.
How beautiful is he, how playful! Full of power and strenght.
All praise be yours, my Lord, through Sister Earth, our mother,
Who feeds us in her sovereignty and produces
Various fruits with colored flowers and herbs.

Everything give praise to God! Praise God through everything! All of creation spoke to him of God, just like the Eucharist spoke to him of Christ and of God. In all the things of the earth he saw the wonderful, the all-powerful, all-wise, all-good Lord and Father. How did Francis sing? How did he teach his friars the music so that they could sing to God the "Canticle of the Creatures"?

The choirs which, especially in Assisi, recreate medieval melodies so splendidly, probably have preserved in some of their songs the melodic themes and the beautiful chants that Francis composed together with the lyrics of that first poem in Italian. And it seems appropriate that this language was born praising God.

Francis' health did not improve during his stay at San Damiano nor would it get any better later on. This worried the vicar Brother Elias, the saint's companions, and even Cardinal Hugoline who, in the end, counseled and gave the order that Francis be moved to Rieti where the papal court was currently located because of a rebellion which had broken out in Rome in April of 1225. The cardinal figured that the pope's doctors would have certainly been able to join forces to come up with something to improve his condition. Francis subjected himself to the "calvary" recommended by his friends who wanted to alleviate his suffering. So, he set out for Rieti, traveling along whatever road and by whatever means of transportation the friars were able to offer or he could endure. He moved along in several brief stages, place by place, village by village, eventually coming closer to Rieti. Sometimes he stayed a while in a village because he would suffer another hemorrhage. He left Terni and finally arrived in the Rieti Valley. He first stopped to visit the priest at St. Fabian's, the place where today is found the friary of La Foresta. From here he moved on to Rieti. Perhaps he also stopped at the house of Theobald Saraceni before continuing his journey to the hermitage of St. Eleutherius. He probably did not ignore the opportunity to spend a couple of days at Greccio to renew the memories of his Christmas scene and also at Fontecolombo which had so many other recollections.

During this period of time the pope's doctors did the best they could, but it was very little. Francis, meanwhile, developed a friendship with them, and he had the chance to say good things to them and to show them some good example. But his illness got worse very quickly. When the doctors realized that their treatments were of no use, they decided to adopt some drastic measures to remedy the situation. Very straightforwardly they proposed to cauterize his temples, that is, to burn the temples with a red-hot iron. This was considered to be a shocking and state-of-the-art therapy. So, they carried it out. Hygiene was not very strict in those days. At the most, anesthesia consisted of some strong drink laced with a sedative.

When Francis felt the heat of the extremely hot poker, he was afraid, just like a child. And he reacted with the simplicity of a child, exclaiming, "Brother Fire, please show me how nice and friendly you are and do not burn me more than I can

220

take!". The fire did not sting that badly. He actually invited the doctors to repeat the operation if it were needed because be did not feel any pain. The friars, meanwhile, ran away because of their fear of the red-hot iron and the stench of the burning flesh.

The doctors realized that all their attempts to find a cure were useless, including the cauterization. They decided to wash their hands of the whole thing and advised the friars to take the ailing Francis to Siena which, at that time, was renowned for its healthy climate. But, apart from some little relief he got from the milder weather, even Siena could not work any miracles on Francis' health.

One night, however, the saint suffered such a violent hemorrhage that he felt he was going to die. He thought about all his friars – those close by and those far away, those of the present day and those of the future – and he did not want to leave them without some sort of last will and testament. He asked Brother Bernard of Prato to get paper and a pen and to write down his final good-byes and his last recommendations. This had to be done very quickly because his death seemed so imminent.

"Write that I bless all my brothers, those who are in the Order, and those who will come until the end of the world. Since, because of my weakness and the pain of my sickness, I am not strong enough to speak, I make known my will to my brothers briefly in these three phases, namely: as a sign that they remember my blessing and my testament, let them always love one another; let them always love and be faithful to our Lady Holy Poverty; and let them always be faithful and subject to the prelates and all clerics of Holy Mother Church" (cf. *Leg. Perug.* 17).

The urgency turned out to be unfounded. Francis recovered a bit and gained back a bit of strength. Brother Elias took advantage of the situation to begin the journey back to Assisi where he had wanted the holy father to bring his life to a close. The first stage of the journey was Celle di Cortona where the group had to stop a while because Francis' condition got worse. It seemed that his abdomen became distended and his legs and feet swelled up. His stomach, moreover, could not hold down food anymore, and at times he was overtaken by intense pain of the spleen and the liver.

Here was poverty reaching its fulfillment.

THE CANTICLE IS COMPLETED

In St. Francis' day it was a rather common practice to steal relics. And, if the relic happened to be the entire body of a famous saint, it was all the more attractive! It is in place to forgive those sorts of people, because during these times of questioning and misgivings – and the thirteenth century was ripe with all this uncertainty – the presence of the body of a saint in a particular city gave the citizenry a certain confidence and acted as a psychologically stabilizing force for the population. The more famous the saint, the more they felt protected. For the ordinary people the saint was some one who was close-by, accessible, and made of the same stuff as themselves. The impression was given, on the other hand, that God was far away and very remote, perhaps because the clergy insisted in their preaching that God was not only a loving Father but also the Master of the Kingdom, a completely other-worldly Spirit almost in total contrast to the "fleshiness" of the human being.

So, then, if the bodies of saints were being stolen, Brother Elias, as soon as Francis was in a condition to continue his journey, decided to lead him to Assisi and to avoid passing near any of the larger population centers, like Perugia. After all, Francis was considered a living relic! Any stop along the way could signify the fortunate location of his passing, and thereby would mean the place which would keep his body and venerate it. If Francis were to pass through Perugia, the citizens of the town would not have passed up the opportunity to use any conceivable excuse to keep him there till he died. For this reason the party would leave Celle di Cortona to accompany the saint, would travel in the direction of Gubbio, and then would pass by Nocera where they met up with a military escort sent just in time from Assisi which took charge of the ailing Francis and accompanied him directly into the city in order to avoid any attack from the people of Nocera or from the citizens of Foligno.

Francis returned to Assisi under a military escort. He would have wanted to arrive back in his own city in a simpler way, one more appropriate for a Friar Minor. By then, however, he realized that he was no longer in charge of his own well being or of the efforts to keep him hidden. Those closest to him, those he trusted the most, in their belief that they were providing for him the highest honor, were really doing him a great injustice. They deprived him of the only willful choice he had left: moving around here and there as God inspired him and as his body permitted him. He who by this time had been marked with the signs of crucifixion and had promised quick and ready obedience to his minister accepted this ultimate deprivation with his usual open-hearted and open-armed spirit.

He reached the city of Assisi where, on account of the occasion, everybody was caught up in the excited frenzy of welcoming back the famous son of the city for the last moments of his life. Still, there was a respectful quiet about town because the people realized that his upcoming death, no matter how glorious, would be such a terrible loss. Francis was being led about. When the rhythm of the donkey's footsteps hit the pavement, the sound reverberated all around, causing the

224

startled faces of the Assisians to turn and move aside. Francis kept his eyes cast down to hide the suffering he was carrying about in his body and to safeguard his humility. He was surrounded by friars and soldiers.

The crowd followed him as far as the bishop's house which was secure enough that Francis could stay there a while. This was a place kept safe against attack because it was within the walls of the city. This was also a religious place where the saint would not mind staying. It was here that he stripped himself of the clothes of Peter Bernardone. It was here that the bishop presented him with the gift of a tunic and a mantle, old as they might have been, to shield his nakedness. Now once again the bishop did something else for him: with the cloak of his veneration and the comfort of his own house he covered the ultimate nakedness of Francis who was no longer in control of even heading in the direction where his heart led him. So there he stayed and rested at the episcopal palace.

Theoretically there is a difference between watching him closely like a prisoner so that he would not be kidnapped from Assisi and keeping a sacred vigil over him day and night so that nobody could carry him away from Assisi. But practically it is the same thing. Neither one of them would allow him to move about as he would like. Francis was not at the bishop's house as a recluse. He was there as a person under protection. He would have wanted to go to the Porziuncula where his friars were waiting for him. The circumstances, however, prevented him from doing that. Consequently, he stayed on with a humble heart, as though he were in a place of the friars. He did not even realize that he was the object of all the people's constant loving attention. Nor was he aware of being the topic of gossip as though he were some newsworthy personage.

One fine day, however, the friars made sure that he took

note of what was happening. Francis did not experience much relief during his sufferings. Prayer and contemplation helped him somewhat to keep going, but they did not take away the need to find something that would alleviate the ordeal of spending day after day in darkness so that his eyes would not be bothered. One day he asked to listen to a bit of music. The friars brought to him a rudimentary, hand-made stringed instrument, and they began to sing the "Canticle of the Creatures" the lyrics of which he had composed at San Damiano and whose melody he also created.

They filled the silence of the palace with music that reverberated through the halls and streamed outside through the doors and windows. It was such a joyous sound, just so appropriate for a canticle of praise for and through all of the creatures which cause the whole earth to rejoice. This song, which had grown out of the immense suffering Francis had endured while at San Damiano, was now bringing intense happiness to the bishop's house and to the whole city. The people who came to the bishop's palace in order to weep and mourn over Francis' imminent death were scandalized by the joyful music. They felt it was out of place in the context of the somber mood of sadness and grief with death just around the corner. It was like wearing a bright red dress at a mournful funeral.

There were and there still are friars and other persons who just cannot bring themselves to conceive of Christianity as a religion of joy and laughter. For these people religion is synonymous with long, sullen faces; they think that anything pleasant or enjoyable is also sinful or, at least, a waste of time.

Somebody finally got to Francis and made him aware of how shocked the people were. "What's with you, Francis? Here the people come, expecting you to be so penitential and sorrowful, to be crying your eyes out as you meditate on your sins. ... And instead there is music all over the place, as if this were a party. You are giving scandal, Francis. Think about how many souls you could be ruining!"

Jesus Christ was also criticized for being too joyful for the tastes of some people during his time.

Brother Elias tried to be very diplomatic about it:

"Dearest Brother, the great joy shown by you and your companions gives me great comfort and edification. But the people of this city venerate you as a saint, and are well aware that you will soon die of your incurable disease; so when they hear the "Praises" sung day and night they are likely to say to themselves, How can this man show so much joy when he is about to die? He ought to be preparing himself for death.'"

Francis replied: "Do you remember the vision that you saw at Foligno, when you told me that it had been revealed to you that I had only two years to live? Before you had this vision, by the grace of God Who implants all good things in our hearts and inspires the words of the faithful, I often meditated upon my end both by day and by night. And after you had that vision, I was even more careful to give daily thought to my death."

Then he continued in great fervor of spirit, "Brother, allow me in my infirmities to 'rejoice in the Lord' and in His praises, for by the grace and assistance of the Holy Spirit I am so united and conjoined to my Lord that by His mercy I may rightly rejoice in Him, the Most High" (*Spec. Perf.* 121).

Nothing more was ever mentioned about it. Francis went on asking for the canticle to be sung, and the good friars continued to sing it for him.

In Assisi not everything was running as smoothly as we would think. The authorities in the city were not in agreement with each other, and hence the people were suffering because of this. One day Francis simply would no longer put up with a situation that had dragged on for far too long. The bishop and the mayor of Assisi not only were not talking to each other any more, but they also stooped to arguing with each other out in public. Bishop Guido, was not an easy man to get along with. He had the enthusiasm of a generous and outgoing person, but he was also very temperamental and thin-skinned, as often is the kind of person who is not accustomed to being defied. The whole thing had erupted into a quarrel which in no way whatsoever edified the people.

It was not that they could be scandalized. In those days the attitudes toward religious authority were very different from ours today. Today we pretend to think of bishops and clergy as angelic, saintly people; and, for this reason, we are appalled as soon as they do not match up the role we have assigned to them. In the Middle Ages, however, the people were more unpretentious: they accepted the liabilities and the assets of the clergy with a much greater sense of realism. They knew, after all, that they were people of this world and made out of the same stuff as every other human being.

Nonetheless, all of this talk about realism did not take away the ill feelings caused by the clash between the highest authorities of the city of Assisi. It was as if in a certain way the harmony and the oneness of his own spirit and body was breaking apart and he could no longer lean on even that to keep his own human balance.

So, he called two of his friars and he sent them to the mayor, requesting, "Brother Francis wants you to come to him." Likewise, two others went to the bishop, asking, "Lord Bishop, Brother Francis would like you to consider going to him. So, in the entrance hall of the bishop's palace, Francis, the bishop, and the mayor all came together. There were also some people around who were interested in seeing what was going to happen.

When the saint gave the signal, like a cantor at a liturgical service, the friars began to sing. People all around listened intently to the lyrics and to the music which broke the silence of that vestibule. The friars chanted:

All praise be yours, my Lord, through those who grant pardon
For love of you; through those who endure sickness and trial.
Happy are those who endure in peace,
By you, Most High, they will be crowned.

Francis did not particularly address himself to either the mayor or to the bishop as individuals. He had called both of them together so that they could participate in this prayer which grew out of his own experience of contemplation. He had seen and encountered God in and through the scorching sun, the water, the wind, and the earth which produces colored flowers and herbs. Up to this point he had not sung about meeting God in other people. The part of the "Canticle" which he had composed so far did not yet make mention of the human person. Now finally he had been able to experience God in and through human beings, if only the bishop and the mayor could be reconciled with each other. As is said: God is never so close to humanity and humanity is never so close to God than when one person forgives another, that is, when someone forgives the suffering caused by the other and bears sickness and trial (the verb Francis actually used means "sustains," which in turn means to "hold up from underneath"; this implies not just "supporting" passively but "carrying the burden" – a Simon of Cyrene activity). God is never so close to humanity!

The mayor and the bishop looked at each other with tears in their eyes, laying aside their pride and opening up their hearts. They approached each other. The mayor knelt before the bishop and asked for forgiveness; the bishop embraced the mayor to make amends with him and with God. Never before had the bishop and the mayor been so close to God.

A knowing smile lit up Francis' face which had been signed with such suffering. This truly was a miracle, and Francis was so happy that he instigated it.

He stayed a little while longer at the bishop's palace. But by then, now that the reconciliation had come about, there was no sense in sticking around. The call of the Porziuncula became stronger and stronger. He longed to get back to his origins, and the people of Assisi no longer had the power or the reasons to stop him from going. Francis was only asking to return to the place where his whole life started.

They prepared a stretcher for him; an armed escort was assigned to him, and the people accompanied him to that gate of the city which looked out over the road and the valley below where St. Mary of the Angels stood. The party set off slowly, carrying the stretcher. As it proceeded along bit by bit, Francis left behind the memories of his own city. That look of Sir Peter Bernardone. The tenderness of Lady Pica. The narrow streets where he played as a child and sang as a teenager. The school of St. George. The store in his house. The public square and the garden walls. How good it all seemed as he looked around this very last time with those eyes which made everything so dimmed and distorted that he could hardly see anything. He knew that he would never again return to Assisi alive.

This is what Doctor Goodjohn said to Francis (who actually nicknamed him "Welcome" because, according to the Gospels, only one alone is good, and that is the Father who is in heaven):

"What do you think about my dropsy?" the saint asked.

"Brother, with the help of God you will get better."

But Francis insisted: "Tell me the truth. What is your opinion? I am not afraid of whatever you tell me because, by the grace of God, I am not a timid sort of person who fears death. I am equally happy whether I live or I die."

So Doctor Welcome said to him: "Father, according to the medical knowledge we now have, your illness is clearly incurable. I think that toward the end of September or in the beginning of October you are going to die."

Francis thought a while and then said: "Welcome, my sister death!" Thinking a while longer, he commanded: "If it be my Lord's pleasure that I should die soon, call me Brother Angelo and Brother Leo, and let them sing to me of Sister Death."

Once again the "Canticle" was sung. At the end, after the stanza praising God in and through those who forgive, Francis added a stanza of praise which almost seemed impossible:

All praise be yours, my Lord, through Sister Death,
From whom no one among the living can escape.
Woe to those who die in mortal sin!
Happy those She finds doing your will!
The second death can do no harm to them.

Then Leo and Angelo concluded the hymn with the old ending:

Praise and bless my Lord, and give him thanks,
And serve him with great humility.
(cf. *Spec. Perf.* 122 and 123).

The party proceeded down the road. At that point where the hillside on which the city stood disappeared into the lowlands of the valley, Francis told those who were carrying him to stop. Also, the military escort came to a stop. He asked to be turned around so that he would be able to see the city of Assisi. So, the bearers turned the stretcher around.

There was Assisi lying before him, flourishing with its pink stone face, looking splendid under the deep green color of Mount Subasio, and outstanding with the fortress on top ruined in the 1198 attack, with its straight walls, and with its imposing belfries rising majestically above the houses. Francis recognized it for its unmistakable topography. If he did not distinguish the towers, though they were not far away, he still could make out the general shape of the city as a whole which, on this beautiful September day in Umbria, Brother

Sun illuminated magnificently and Sister Weather made the air so clean and clear that even trees far away could be distinguished right away. This is the very same September view that I now enjoy as I sit at my desk and watch the whole vista unfold before me out my window.

"Lord, it is said that in former days this city was the haunt of wicked men." (Francis was praying out loud, as if to let the very stones of the town hear every word.) "But now it is clear that out of your infinite mercy and in your own time you have been pleased to shower special and abundant favors upon it. From your goodness alone you have chosen it for yourself, that it may become the home and dwelling of those who know you in truth and glorify your holy name, and spread abroad the fragrance of a good report, of holy life, of true doctrine, and of evangelical perfection to all Christian people. I therefore beseech you, O Lord Jesus Christ, Father of mercies, that you will not remember our ingratitude, but ever be mindful of your abundant compassion which you have shown towards it, that it may ever be the home and dwelling-place of those who know you in truth and glorify your blessed and most glorious name for ever and ever. Amen" (*Spec. Perf.* 124).

And then he added: "May you be blessed by the Lord, City of Assisi, because he has chosen you to be the homeland and the dwelling-place of all those who recognize God, glorify God in truth, and want to honor God's name."

He stayed there enraptured and speechless.

The friars delicately turned the stretcher around, and the group continued its journey toward St. Mary of the Angels. Nobody said a thing, not even any of the soldiers who made up the escort.

They were afraid that they might cancel out the words of Francis prayer on that bright September day toward sunset.

THE EVENING PRAYER OF THE SKYLARKS

When the party arrived at St. Mary of the Angels, the friars who lived there all came out of their huts to welcome their father who had come down from Assisi to meet Sister Death at the place where he began to live the idea that had now become their way of life. They escorted him under the trees to the tiny church of St. Mary's. They stayed outside so that Francis, who was lying on the bier, could spend some time by himself in the little chapel which was so precious to him. From his little bed Francis adored the Eucharist placed with such care in the tabernacle, and he greeted the Virgin Mary:

"Hail, O Lady,
holy Queen,
Mary, holy Mother of God:
you are the virgin made church
and the one chosen by the most holy Father in heaven
whom He consecrated
with His most holy beloved Son
and with the Holy Spirit the Paraclete,
in whom there was and is
all the fullness of grace and every good.
Hail, His Palace!

Hail, His Tabernacle!
Hail, His Home!
Hail, His Robe!
Hail, His Servant!
Hail, His Mother!
And, hail all you holy virtues
which through the grace and light of the Holy Spirit are poured into the hearts of the faithful so that from their faithless state you may make them faithful to God."

When he finished praying and his half-blind eyes filled with tears as he recalled all the warm memories of that place, the friars transported his dying body to a little cell of stone and thatched hay not far from there so that he could listen and take part when the friars sang Lauds and Matins and Vespers, praising the wonders of the Lord God. The cell was all in order as though it were already set up as the shrine famous throughout the world for welcoming the last breath of Francis. As far as it was possible, the cell was kept darkened, so as not to affect his eyes too much. The friars kept watch around him. Even the soldiers made arrangements to stay there for a while – short or long they did not know.

Francis was very much aware that his death was very near. Before he died, however, he wanted, as best be could, to take care of those things he was responsible for. He wanted to commend his body to the earth, but he did not want to leave behind any unfinished business or regrets. Even though he was no longer the minister general, he still was the father and the guide of all those people who followed him and who were now scattered all over the world. He brought to mind once again the things that were most important to him and dedicated some time to thinking about each one of them. He had already sent a letter to Clare and the sisters at San Damiano, giving them his blessing and his encouragement.

234

This letter was probably handed down, and we know of it through a thirteenth-century document preserved in the Poor Clare Monastery of Novaglie near Verona:

"Listen, little poor ones called by the Lord,
who have come together from many parts and provinces:
Live always in truth,
that you may die in obedience.
Do not look at the life outside,
for that of the Spirit is better.
I beg you through great love,
to use with discernment
the alms which the Lord gives you.
Those who are weighed down by sickness
and the others who are wearied because of them,
all of you: bear it in peace.
For you will sell this fatigue at a very high price
and each one of you will be crowned queen
in heaven with the Virgin Mary."

Francis sent a friar from the Porziuncula to San Damiano to reassure the sisters that they would certainly have the opportunity to see him again in a way that God would provide. Without a doubt this would give them great consolation.

After Clare, toward whom he had taken on a particular commitment to look after, he thought of friars whom he knew and all those, so many of them, whom he would never see either now or in the future. While thinking in his little hut among the trees of the Porziuncula, he decided to leave them a last will and testament. He would not write it in a hurry, as he did with the one dictated in Siena when there seemed to be the urgency of imminent death. This time, however, it would be unfrenzied, determined, reflective, and yet very much full of life. It had to be the last word to the brothers, and, for this reason, he thought he would write a testament that could bring together in one text the best of all his experiences, both his dreams for tomorrow and his real concerns for today.

He started off by recalling his first personal experience together with his first aspiration:

"The Lord granted me, Brother Francis, to begin to do penance in this way: While I was in sin, it seemed very bitter to me to see lepers. And the Lord himself led me among them and I had mercy upon them. And when I left them, that which seemed bitter to me was changed into sweetness of soul and body; and afterward I lingered a little and left the world" (1-3).

The thought of those miserable days when he did not even have a house in which he could lay down his head brought him to think about the house of God:

"And the Lord gave me such faith in churches that I would simply pray and speak in this way: 'We adore you, Lord Jesus Christ, in all your churches throughout the world, and we bless you, for through your holy cross you have redeemed the world'" (4-5).

Along with God and with the Body of Christ which he adored in the churches, he remembered the priests with respect as long as they were living in union with Rome:

"Afterward the Lord gave me and still gives me such faith in priests who live according to the manner of the holy Roman Church because of their order, that if they were to persecute me, I would still have recourse to them. And if I possessed as much wisdom as Solomon had and I came upon pitiful priests of this world, I would not preach contrary to their will in the parishes in which they live. And I desire to fear, love, and honor them and all others as my masters. And I do not wish to consider sin in them because I discern the Son of God in them and they are my masters. And I act in this way since I see nothing corporally of the most High Son of God in this world except His Most holy Body and Blood why they receive and which they alone minister to others" (6-10).

To think about priests was just like thinking about the eucharistic Christ for whom Francis had such an attentive tenderness. He was deeply committed to the Eucharist and to anything that pertained to Christ because, as he had seen, frequently there was just too much neglect and carelessness. As he reflected on this, he went on to say:

"And these most holy mysteries I wish to have honored above all things and to be reverenced and to have them reserved in precious places. Wherever I come upon His most holy written words in unbecoming places, I desire to gather them up and I ask that they be collected and placed in a suitable place... And we should honor and respect all theologians and those who minister the most holy divine words as those who minister spirit and life to us" (11-13).

Francis had made a profession of faith by remembering what he had cherished the most as a source of inspiration and as a guide. Now he could let himself convey the good memories about the first steps along that new path he embarked upon.

"And after the Lord gave me brothers, no one showed me what I should do, but the Most High Himself revealed to me that I should live according to the form of the Holy Gospel. And I had this written down simply and in a few words and the Lord Pope confirmed it for me" (14-15).

Francis was so fascinated by that way of living the Gospel which Christ demonstrated to his disciples. His friars, who now had that form codified in a rule of life, would be reminded that the rule was only meant to be the legal translation of his original ambition. They were supposed to respect it and interpret it by always keeping in mind that "form of the Holy Gospel" which the Holy Father approved. Just as the rule had to be interpreted in the light of the "form of the Holy Gospel," so must life in community bear the mark of at least that free-spiritedness and enthusiasm which was characteristic of the early days. This is why Francis took such great pains to describe those first experiences:

"And those who came to receive life gave to the poor everything which they were capable of possessing and they were content with one tunic, patched inside and out, with a cord and short trousers. And we had no desire for anything more. We who were clerics used to say the Office as other clerics did; the lay brothers said the Our Father; and we quite willingly stayed in churches. And we were simple and subject to all.

"And I used to work with my hands, and I still desire to work; and I firmly wish that all my brothers give themselves to honest work. Let those who do not know how to work learn, not from desire of receiving wages for their work but as an example and in order to avoid idleness. And when we are not paid for our work, let us have recourse to the table of the Lord, seeking alms from door to door. The Lord revealed to me a greeting, as we used to say: 'May the Lord give you peace'" (16-23).

Francis began each new sentence with the word *"And"* ("et" in Latin). This gave a certain staccato rhythm to the flow of his memories which would cause him to stop and reflect a bit; then he would start talking again.

When he finished recalling his memories, he returned to the present situation. There was nothing left for him to say in his Testament regarding those beginning years of his life, not even the papal approval of the rule which he considered as very important. So, from those early memories he passed right on to today's concerns. Reality for him was a bit sad because the 1223 Rule was not being observed as fully as it could have been. This upset Francis very much. At the very least, the friars could have observed what they had obligated themselves to follow by virtue of their vows and promises! Faced with such disregard and negligence, Francis unexpectedly comes across in a severe and stinging manner that we are not accustomed to seeing.

At this point of the Testament, the tone changes, and Francis seems to take the position of rising above the others and acting as the minister general. It was as though he were saying: even though you have made your preference known for a minister general to guide you along the gospel way of life which you have chosen, freely as brothers, nonetheless I myself am going to talk to you now as the minister general in behalf of the rule which clearly spells out your rights and duties and indicates who is the superior and who is the subject. So he continues:

"Let the brothers beware that they by no means receive churches or poor dwellings or anything which is built for them, unless it is in harmony with that holy poverty which we have promised in the Rule, and let them always be guests there as pilgrims and strangers. And I firmly command all of the brothers through obedience that, wherever they are, they should not be so bold as to seek any letter from the Roman Curia either personal, or through an intermediary, neither for a church or for some other place or under the guise of preaching or even for the persecution of their bodies; but wherever they have not been received, let them flee into another country to do penance with the blessing of God" (24-26).

That he said this at all meant that there truly was a need for him to mention it.

Another serious problem in the Order that he had confronted was the friars' disobedience toward their superiors. In the Testament he offers his own example and summons everyone to a certain kind of observance just as he calls to task those discontent friars who disobeyed liturgical norms. He was particularly worried about those who might have had to separate themselves from the orthodoxy of the Catholic faith. The Catholic identity of Order was a very important value for him. He was so concerned about this that he established precise and strict regulations regarding those who drifted away. Actually the exactness of the norms the friars were to follow when they came upon someone who was not living as a Catholic seem almost childish. But this kind of "childishness" on his part is a clear sign of how concerned Francis really was and how wrong any one is who holds the opinion that Francis was oppressed by the Roman Curia and was robbed of his spontaneity. He goes on to say:

"And I firmly wish to obey the minister general of this fraternity and another guardian whom it might please him to give me. And I wish to be so captive in his hands that I cannot go anywhere or do anything beyond obedience and his will, for he is my master.

"And although I may be simple and infirm, I wish nonetheless always to have a cleric who will celebrate the Office for me as it is contained in the Rule. And all the other brothers are bound to obey their guardians and to celebrate the Office according to the Rule. And if any are found who do not celebrate the Office according to the Rule and who wish to alter it in any way or who are not Catholics, let all the brothers be obliged through obedience that wherever they come upon such a brother, they must bring him to the custodian who is nearest to that place where they have found him. And the custodian is strictly bound through obedience to guard him strongly as a prisoner day and night, so that he cannot be snatched from his hands until he can personally deliver him into the hands of his minister. And the minister is strictly bound through obedience to send him with brothers who shall guard him as a prisoner day and night until they deliver him before the Lord of Ostia who is the master, protector, and corrector of the entire fraternity.

"And let the brothers not say: this is another Rule; because this is a remembrance, an admonition, and exhortation, and my testament, which I, little Brother Francis, prepare for all of you, my blessed brothers, so that we may observe in a more Catholic manner the Rule which we have promised to the Lord" (27-34).

His barrage of heated admonitions calmed down and turned into an embrace of his brothers, just like the refreshing serenity that follows a storm. Nonetheless, he still wanted to counsel the friars about some other things:

"And the minister general and all other ministers and custodians are bound through obedience not to add or to subtract from these words. And let them always have this writing with them along with the Rule. And in all the chapters which they hold, when they read the Rule, let them also read these words. And I through obedience strictly command all my brothers, cleric and lay, not to place glosses on the Rule or on these words, saying: They are to be understood in this way. But as the Lord has granted me to speak and to write the Rule and these words simply and purely, so shall you understand them simply and without gloss, and observe them with their holy manner of working until the end" (35-39).

He had no more admonitions to make. The last one in which he commanded the friars not to "place glosses" on the rule was an appeal to their maturity and their freedom. He knew well that, if there were any sort of commentaries, they would be juridical explanations or legal norms on what they had to do and what they did not have to do. That would not please Francis at all. Even though the rule put some order and organization to his ideals, still it was pristine and preserved a good part of his earliest aspirations. At least this they ought not to spoil with normative prescriptions.

Francis was getting very tired now. All that was left was a blessing – generous and full of affection – for the friars of the present and of the future.

And for me.

In this last paragraph it is as though he chants the benediction:

"And may whoever shall have observed these things be filled in heaven with the blessing of the most high Father and on earth with the blessing of His beloved Son with the most Holy Spirit the Paraclete and with all the powers of heaven and all the saints. And I, little brother Francis, your servant, inasmuch as I can, confirm for you this most holy blessing both within and without" (40-41).

Francis was absorbed in contemplation. By now he had made provisions for his friars to keep his memory alive and to have his Testament which would serve as their examination of conscience and would help them imagine what those early days filled with such fervor were really like.

During those days, as he prepared himself to die, there was, besides Clare and the friars, somebody else he wanted to remember. By leaving a final word, he wanted to make everyone very aware that he or she was significant enough not to be forgotten. So, he also remembered and pledged himself to Lady Poverty who was for him a real lady. Also, he paid tribute to the other virtues which with the flair of chivalry he imagined as real persons:

"Hail, Queen Wisdom, may the Lord protect you with your sister, holy pure Simplicity.

Lady, holy Poverty, may the Lord protect you with your sister, holy Humility.

Lady, holy Charity, may the Lord protect you with your sister, holy Obedience.

O most holy Virtues, may the Lord protect all of you, from whom you come and proceed."

It was his wish that poverty would reign supreme in the place where he died. He knew that these final days would be considered as sources of great inspiration and as opportunities for solid advice. This is why he did not stop with just the mention of poverty.

Francis was very adept at utilizing dramatic instances to make sure in the most effective way possible that a person did not forget what was experienced. He did not want a habit which he could say was his own; and he wanted to be placed naked on the ground when Sister Death was truly close at hand. So his own guardian gave him a habit in charity and made him promise that he would not give it away to someone else. The friars would remember this scene vividly and would hand on the message of the event with much greater success than any discourse or sermon could do.

He also remembered the church of the Porziuncula which was right there just a few paces away. He even wanted to dramatize his attachment to it by having them carry him there to die. The Legend of Perugia says this about the Porziuncula:

"We who lived with blessed Francis bear witness that he said with great insistence 'Of all the churches in the world that the blessed Virgin loves, she bears the greatest love for this one.' He spoke in this way because of the numerous prerogatives given by God to this friary and because this had been revealed to him in that very place. That is why during all his life, he bore a great devotion and a great respect for this place. And so that the memory of it would remain engraved in the hearts of the brothers, he wished, as his death was drawing near, to have it written down in his testament that the brothers should do likewise. In fact when he was near death, he said before the minister general and the other brothers: 'I wish to make arrangements regarding the friary of the Porziuncula and leave them as a testament to my brothers so that this place will always be treated by them with great reverence and devotion" (9).

In the Testament which we described above there is no trace of this remembrance. We can consider Francis' exhortation as one of those word-of-mouth additions to fill out what he had already put into writing. The tiny church, however, was able to be the right place for the renewal of the friars, whenever they would have the desire to return to their roots. In fact, Francis said:

"See to it, my sons, that you never abandon this place. If you are driven out from one side, go back in at the other. For this place is truly holy and is the dwelling place of God. Here, when we were but a few, the Most High gave us increase; here he enlightened the hearts of his poor ones by the light of his wisdom; here he set our wills afire with the fire of his love. Here he who prays with a devout heart will obtain what he prays for and he who offends will be punished more severely" (1 *Cel.* 106).

Francis was a sensitive person. Once he found a friend, he loved him deeply and would never forget him. During those interminable hours, memories took hold of him. He recalled Bernard's enthusiasm, Peter's conversion, Giles' simplicity, and all those people he met along the way.

He also remembered the Roman noblewoman to whom he had given the name "Brother Jacopa" and who was considered very much a part of his spiritual family. Once, while he was in Rome, he gave her a lamb which someone had given to him as a gift because he did not have the heart to kill it. This lamb in turn became a legend around Rome because of his fondness for it.

When he thought of Jacopa, he remembered the little

sweet spice cakes she used to make. He wished he had some of them right at that moment. Even though his stomach would not hold anything, perhaps he could keep down some of those.

Such moments of tenderness were good for his spirits. He felt the need to have his dearest friends close at hand. He wanted to touch them. He wanted to bless them. He asked that Brother Bernard be called to his side, and he came right away. He sat down close to the dying saint and said:

"'Father, I beg you to bless me and give me some sign of affection, for if you show your paternal love towards me, I am sure that God Himself and the brethren will love me more.'

Blessed Francis could not see him, because he had already lost the sight of his eyes many days before; but he reached out his right hand and laid it on the head of Brother Giles, the third of the friars, thinking that he was laying it on the head of Brother Bernard, who was sitting beside him. Immediately aware of this through the Holy Spirit, he said, 'This is not the head of my Brother Bernard.' Then Brother Bernard came closer, and laying his hands on his head, blessed Francis gave him his blessing. Then he said to one of his companions, 'Write down what I tell you. Brother Bernard was the first friar that the Lord gave me, and he was first to observe the absolute perfection of the Gospel by giving all his property to the poor. Because of this, and because of his many other merits, I cannot help loving him more than any other friar in the whole Order. As far as I may, I therefore desire and decree that whoever becomes Minister General is to love and honor him as they would myself. Let the Minister and all the friars of the Order regard him as taking my place" (*Spec. Perf.* 107).

After blessing Bernard, Francis had the friars write to Brother Jacopa. He dictated the letter, and asked one of them to set out right away to take it to Rome. The letter read:

"You should know, my dear one, that the blessed Christ,

through his grace has revealed to me that the end of my life is very near. So, if you would want to see me alive, you should hurry right away to St. Mary of the Angels, as soon as you receive this letter. Because, if you do not come during these days, you will not find me alive. And please bring with you some sackcloth to wrap my body and some candles for my funeral. Also I ask you to bring me some of that special food which you used to give me when I was in Rome."

The text of the letter, as we hear it, is doubtful.

Jacopa, however, had already been informed. And so, before the friar could even set off on the journey to deliver the letter, the Lady, with her family and her bodyguards as escorts, was already there at St. Mary of the Angels. And she did bring the sackcloth and the candles for the funeral. And, of course, those little spice cakes called "sweet mostaccioli." Most of all, she brought a heart filled with tenderness.

Francis let her in at once, even though she was a woman and the place was off limits to women.

Now that he was very near death, Francis took the opportunity to demonstrate that his sanctity was not sour and dour, full of deprivation and prohibitions, as a certain hagiography would like to make us believe. He loved to sing, even if this caused a bit of scandal. He asked for that sweet confection. He longed to see a certain woman again even to the point of letting her into a place where she was not allowed to go. In my opinion, this man deserves to be studied more carefully. His holiness is much more encompassing that it may seem at first glance.

Francis was now at peace on the inside. He had put in order all his sentiments, and had carried out what he felt he immediately had to do. The only thing left for him to accomplish was to approach his own death with great consciousness and love.

His day-to-day living was simplified as much as he wanted; his suffering body became his cell in which he prayed intently and recollected himself deeply. Every now and then he would utter a word, give a blessing, or invite the friars to praise the Lord. His impending but delayed death was like a piece of advice on how to live in union with God and with the brothers. At a certain point, "the holy father commanded that bread be brought to him. He blessed and broke it and gave a small piece to each one to eat. Commanding also that a book of the Gospels be brought, he asked that the Gospel according to St. John be read to him from the place that begins: 'Before the feast of the Passover'" (2 Cel. 217).

When it was time for Vespers on the evening of October third, Francis developed a fever and he grew very weak, like a flame that flickers on a wick which is almost out of oil. He wanted to be placed on the ground, and he asked the friars to sing. He sang along with them. They chanted Psalm 142 which speaks of that longing to go to God:

"With all my voice I cry to you, Yahweh;
with all my voice I entreat you.
I pour out my complaint before you;
I tell you all my distress.
When my spirit faints within me,
you, Yahweh, know my path.
On the way where I shall walk
they have hidden a snare to trap me.
I look on my right and see:
there is no one who takes my part.
I have lost all means of escape,
there is no one who cares for my life.
I cry to you, Yahweh,
I have said: 'You are my refuge,
all I have in the land of the living.'
Listen, then, to my cry,
for I am in the depth of distress.

Rescue me from those who pursue me,
for they are too strong for me."

When the friars, caught up in the melody, joined
their voices to sing

"Bring my soul out of this prison,
and then I shall praise your name.
Around me the just will gather
because of your goodness to me."
Francis left his body on the earth and passed away.

The singing faded out and came to a stop. The friars'
mouths could only recite the "Glory be to the Father, and to
the Son, and to the Holy Spirit" at the conclusion of the
psalm amid their tears and emotions.

The hut became silent. All around it seemed that nature
had quieted down.

Then all of a sudden a "Glory be" burst forth from the
throats of a whole flock of skylarks which were nearby and
around and up·above the hut. They were beginning their war-
ble at vesper time in the evening. They looked like a chorus of
Friars Minor dressed in brown with a capuche on their heads.

It was Saturday, the third of October, in the year 1226.

REPORTING TO ST. FRANCIS

If I decided to write about you, Francis, I did it because I felt I had understood something. I heard the echo of your voice which finally reached my ears after the length of many centuries. I tried to discover some of your experiences in the written pages of your biographers and in some of the aspects of my own experiences, after studying the words you left for us and inquiring about the things people said of you. Since writing this book was like meeting you personally and reporting on that timeless dialogue, I would like to say that you are the Francis whom I recognize as the guidepost for my journey through life.

When you died, all the friars around you were trying to take in that last breath you breathed. I was there too, hidden in the flow of centuries yet to come, to receive that blessing which you left for us across the ups and downs of time.

Here they are, Francis, coming down from Assisi. They are overcome with emotion over the news of your death. Some of them pick the last flowers which they can still find in the fields. Others are carrying olive branches. They are all descending on the Porziuncula. Some are walking slowing, others rather quickly. Some are traveling on horseback, others in carts. They are arriving to see you and to pick you up and carry you back to the city you wanted to leave in order to die where your whole wonderful experiment was born.

The poor, whom you loved so much, are there. The lords and ladies, whom you had wanted to at least be poor in spirit are there too. So are the mayor and the bishop whom you brought back together in reconciliation; they are friends again, as you would have wanted to see them be.

They would not have come down the hill to view your corpse if they still had hate in their hearts. You were the winner, Francis. Or perhaps it is better to say that Christ won this one with you as the means to make it happen.

They are all coming to the hut made of stone and wattle. How many shacks like this would ordinarily merit a visit from the high and mighty! Anyway, they are coming to your cell. Is that not already an accomplishment, Francis?

Here they arrive, and as they stand before you they are not quite sure whether they should pray for you or to you, whether they should say "Eternal rest..." or whether they should ask you to intercede for them. They do not know if they should wear black in mourning or red in celebration. The bishop does not know if he ought to put on the black stole for a funeral or the white one to commemorate the feast of a saint. Francis, this time you have really sent them into a dither! All the real Christians confound the people who are wise in the ways of the world. And you are such a Christian. You are profoundly a follower of Christ. This marvelous name is the only one you added to "John" (the one given to you by your mother at your baptism) and to "Francis" (the one your father carried back for you from France). Nobody ought to add any other name to your "John-Francis" than the one that comes from Christ himself: Christian.

Now almost all of Assisi is gathered down here at St. Mary of the Angels. Also the people of Spello and Foligno and Perugia are here. There are so many people, and it is hard for everyone to see you because you seem so tiny, drowned in that good-sized habit which Father Guardian gave you out of charity. They have carried your body inside the Porziuncula, but the place is much too small for all the people.

And now from the Porziuncula they pick you up to move you to Assisi. Perhaps when I die, they will also bring me to the Porziuncula, as we are used to doing, following your lead.

As the procession snakes along, everybody is singing.

They are carrying your body in great jubilation. I think there is even a cardinal in his bright red robes walking in front of you to honor you. It is quite a privilege to pay you honor, and it is something which helps take away the grief we feel deep inside.

The road they are taking is not the one that runs straight to Assisi; that is, the one you took when you left the city for the last time. They are using the road that detours over toward San Damiano where the Poor Ladies – Clare and her companions – are praying all the time; they are weeping and are longing to see you again just one more time before your mortal remains are lowered into the tomb. You did promise them this!

The Poor Ladies of San Damiano did not come out onto the street. Your body was carried on its bier into the church so that they could behold you and bring to mind your words, your preaching with the ashes, your "Canticle of the Creatures." They are going to notice the wounds caused by the stigmata. Now you are not hiding them anymore. On the back of your hands there is now a black clot of blood which looks like the head of a nail. Now that Clare knows that she can do you no harm, she pretends to place a kiss on your hand and tries to remove that skin which looks like a blood clot. But her efforts are in vain. It is little consolation.

After the stop at San Damiano, you finally re-enter your beloved city. They have prepared a sarcophagus for you in the crypt of the Church of St. George. Do you still remember the place? That is where you learned how to read and write.

We are so sad because we feel deprived of you. It is true that our faith tells us that we have not lost you but that you are even closer to us than before. Yet... Yet it is hard for us to go on without knowing exactly what you are thinking right from your own spoken words.

You know something? You were right when you said that Cardinal Hugoline would become the pope. Pope Honorius met up with you in heaven on March eighteenth. Only five months passed since you died. To take his place, the cardinals elected Hugoline of the Counts of Segni, and he took the name of Gregory IX. He is a decisive sort of fellow, and he has already clashed with the emperor. They are arguing among themselves about some political problems and about some human misunderstandings. Emperor Frederick II incurred excommunication because he did not want to commit himself to the crusade. He was more interested in domestic issues instead of foreign policy. Because of this conflict Pope Gregory had to flee Rome. As luck would have it, he took up residence near Assisi. Did you call him there?

By this time all the people wanted you declared a saint. The pope opened the process of canonization in Perugia on June 13, 1227, not even a year after your death. The process sped along quickly. The witnesses recalled everything, and there were so many of them! And there were so many miracles! They were already writing your biography.

On the twenty-eighth of June the emperor sailed for the east. The pope was put at ease.

Francis, your day finally arrived! I know that, when you

take everything into account, it is really not that important to you. But for us it is a glorious day.

April 16, 1228. The public square is crowded with people. The college of cardinals is assembled. A beautiful liturgical Office has been prepared for you. So many people have requested the honor of putting their hand to this great project. There is even a king in the square. Usually you are not one to take a liking to the high and mighty of this earth, but this particular king would not have given you any trouble. He is a king more in name than in fact. It is John of Brienne, the King of Jerusalem. You would certainly like this title because you see Jesus everywhere.

Then there is your friend the pope. He started the whole thing off with a marvelous discourse that began with the words, "just like the morning star..." You are that morning star he is referring to.

On the nineteenth of July from Perugia he sent throughout the world an official decree entitled "Mira circa nos," which was overflowing with admiration for you. This decree announced to the world that you had been declared a saint.

Well, Francis, pray for us now. Pray for Pope Gregory, for John of Brienne, for the cardinals and bishops, for all your friars, for all the people. Pray also for Frederick II who is actually sailing east to take part in the crusade. We know that on September seventh he will land in Akko with the intention of signing a peace treaty with Melek-el-Khamil.

We know you, Francis, and we know that you did not like the crusaders using their weapons. So I have a question for you: Was it Frederick's intention to make peace for his own advantage and benefit, or perhaps did you in your saintly way help him during that long voyage at sea to gradually turn his heart to thoughts of peace?

Now that I have spoken with you and have told your story,

would you, Francis, like to go along with us and make history? I am sure you would enjoy living and working with us! I am going to try, if you do not mind, to read about you yet again and to study the details of your life once more. If I can manage to present you and describe you to our world by means of my words, you then can speak to us about Jesus Christ. This is the thing that is most important.

TABLE OF CONTENTS